THE SINGER AS INTERPRETER:
CLAIRE CROIZA'S
MASTER CLASSES

THE SINGER AS INTERPRETER:
CLAIRE CROIZA'S
MASTER CLASSES

Edited and translated by

BETTY BANNERMAN

with Notes & Discography by
Patrick Saul

LONDON
VICTOR GOLLANCZ LTD
1989

First published in Great Britain 1989
by Victor Gollancz Ltd
14 Henrietta Street, London WC2E 8QJ

British Library Cataloguing in Publication Data
Bannerman, Betty
    The singer as interpreter: Claire Croiza's master classes
    1. Singing. Theories of Croiza, Claire,
    1822–1946
    I. Title II. Abraham, Hélène. Un art de
    l'interprétation Claire Croiza
    784.9'3

ISBN 0–575–04391–1

NOTE
These Master Classes have been taken and translated
from *Un art de l'interprétation Claire Croiza* by
Hélène Abraham, copyright Hélène Abraham
1954, published privately in Paris, 1954.
The material is used by permission of
the executors of Claire Croiza.

Typeset at The Spartan Press Ltd
Lymington, Hants
and printed in Great Britain by
St Edmundsbury Press Ltd, Bury St Edmunds, Suffolk

ACKNOWLEDGEMENTS

My grateful thanks are due to Claire Croiza's son Jean-Claude Honegger who has provided me with his mother's photographs, letters, programmes and records, together with details of her talks and expressions of appreciation by eminent composers and poets in France, Belgium, Geneva and London, since her death in 1946; and for his permission to translate and publish Croiza's Master Classes ('Causeries').

To the late Hélène Abraham for her book, *Un art de l'interprétation Claire Croiza* that included transcripts of the Master Classes, material that is now the property of Jean-Claude Honegger; to the late Martin Cooper, C.B.E., the author of *French Music*, who generously and patiently edited my translations with the exception of additions to those recitatives in *Orpheus* that I studied with Croiza; to Christopher Underwood who has helped with the final stages and 'order' of the book, and has given encouragement and perception of the continuing value of Croiza's teaching for succeeding generations of his students at the Royal Northern College of Music since he took over the French song class there; to Patrick Saul for his Notes and Discography; to Livia Gollancz for her skilful vetting of the typescript; to Jean-Michel Nectoux's beautiful exhibition, 'Hommage à Claire Croiza', at the Bibliothèque Nationale in Paris in 1984 and the accompanying article in *Revue de la Bibliothèque Nationale*, No. 12 (Summer, 1984); and finally, by no means least, to my husband for his unfailing support.

B.B.

CONTENTS

FOREWORD

This text consists of a translation of some of Claire Croiza's Master Classes from the 1930s, when she lectured on many of the central themes concerning the art of singing and interpretation, with particular reference to the French composers for whom she had been the chosen interpreter.

The reader will find, in the chapter entitled 'Recollections', details of Claire Croiza's early career, in particular at La Monnaie in Brussels, and elsewhere during the First World War. The stage of her career with which this book is chiefly concerned was her work as a singer with composers who chose and admired her as an interpreter of their songs. They included Duparc, Fauré, Debussy, Bréville, Caplet, Roussel, Milhaud and Honegger. It was not only composers who enthused about her performances. Painters and poets were struck by her beautiful presence, her penetrating glance, her unforgettable speaking voice and her delicious sense of wit and humour. Her recitals of music and poetry were very special occasions, and the poets Valéry and Claudel invited her to read their poems at their lectures. Because of her intimate knowledge of how these composers and poets wished their works to be performed, she was asked to give classes at the Ecole Normale de Musique in Paris. In the late 1920s and all through the 1930s, she gave her own public Master Classes at the Salle Chopin and Salle Debussy in Paris, but also at Geneva, Lyons, London and Brussels. In addition, from 1933 to 1938 she gave summer courses at various resorts by the sea or in the mountains.

In 1954 Mme Hélène Abraham published her book, *Un art de l'interprétation: Claire Croiza*, which was based on Croiza's public Master Classes that Mme Abraham had taken down in short-hand as they occurred. Croiza gave her approval to these accounts. For people who read French easily this book was a boon. The diary form in which it is written caused no problems when Croiza was speaking on a general theme, or on the women's rôles in nine operas (see chapter ten). To find her remarks, however, on individual songs, needs constant reference to the index (in the case of Debussy 46 times, of Fauré 43 times and so on). I do not believe that many students would be prepared to do this and, in any case, for English speaking singers a translation is essential. So, in these translations, I have pieced together the various comments on each song, while endeavouring to keep the informal character of these public 'talks'. Croiza liked to refer to them as 'causeries' as they followed after the singing of students at her classes, and she always spoke without notes. I have also included notes from manuscripts sent to me by her son, and also from my own lessons with her, which took place during two months of each year, over a period of ten years.

The inspiration for this book has come from a growing awareness of the value of Mme Croiza's thoughts and views, not only as they were put into practice in her own performances, but also as they have proved themselves of lasting benefit for myself and for other singers and teachers in subsequent work with students of singing at the Northern School of Music and later the Royal Northern College of Music, where the French Song Class which I was asked to establish is being continued by Mr Christopher Underwood.

RECOLLECTIONS OF CLAIRE CROIZA
by Betty Bannerman

CLAIRE CROIZA WAS born in the Avenue de l'Opéra in Paris
on 14 September 1882. Her father, Colonel John Townsend
Connolly, was an American of Irish origin, amply endowed
with this world's goods, who settled in Paris and married a
charming Italian. Claire, the youngest of three children, was a
happy fusion of the Latin and the Celt. Her parents were
artistic, loved music and had knowledge and appreciation of
beautiful things. Claire was an extremely sensitive child and,
to her parents' delight, at a very early age showed that she was
musically gifted to an unusual degree. She learnt the piano and
solfège with great facility, read music fluently and sang like a
lark. She was taken to picture galleries, museums and to
concerts, and began to use her critical faculties very early. But
when she was eighteen her father died suddenly, and it was
unexpectedly found necessary for her to adopt a career.

By this time her voice had developed into a lovely, warm
mezzo-soprano, Italian in character and with an unusually
beautiful timbre; the facility with which she vocalized made it
rather difficult, in her case, to determine the exact label which
people like to affix to a voice. Her teachers, Mlle Revello and
Monsieur Maton, sent her to Jean de Reszke for advice, and
after a few lessons he arranged an audition for her and she was
engaged by the Opéra at Nancy to create the part of Messaline
in de Lara's opera of that name. She never had acting lessons —
she did not need them — but she had learnt to move freely on
the stage, and her whole person was harmonious. She made of
the name-part in this opera — which was not quite a character
'pour les jeunes filles' — a charming, pure young girl straight

out of the convent; she used no make-up at all until her director told her that she must at least make up her eyes, so that they could be seen. The young ladies of Nancy were taken in shoals by their mothers to see this unusual débutante.

Her success was immediate, and it is interesting for us to note that the next year she sang the Angel in the first performance in Paris of Elgar's *The Dream of Gerontius*, conducted by Chevillard. She had taken the name of Croiza as being more suitable for the stage than her own name of Connolly. The critics singled her out, and in 1907, in spite of her youth, she was engaged to sing the leading mezzo rôles at the Théâtre de la Monnaie in Brussels, one of the leading opera houses in Europe at that time. There followed eight years of sensational triumph. Brussels was at her feet, in a way we here can hardly imagine. The students unharnessed the horses from her carriage and dragged it from the opera house back to her hotel, the painters, sculptors and poets were as enthusiastic as the musicians, and her directors were assured of a full house whenever she sang. She gave 68 performances in the first two years.

Not only was her singing exceptionally musical, but she was beautiful, with dark hair over a wide brow, brilliant dark eyes flecked with gold, an extremely mobile and sensitive mouth, and a fascinating personality. On the stage the distinction of her appearance made an immediate and un-forgettable impression. She did not use any of the conven-tional tricks of the operatic stage. The critics wrote of her 'penetrating glance expressing an ardent instinct with an exceptional faculty of emotion and a rich generosity of temperament controlled by a faultless taste'. In Bizet's *Carmen* she looked like a Goya stepping out of its frame, and the painter Bastien made many charming sketches of her Charlotte in Massenet's *Werther*. As Dido in Berlioz's *The Trojans* we are told that she expressed 'the deepest pathos with the utmost sobriety of means . . . and achieved the grandeur of antiquity with an incomparable beauty of line'.

At her own request, the directors of the Monnaie revived

Gluck's *Orpheus* for her and she gave ten performances to packed houses that season. Her Orpheus was a young, virile god — to many the ideal of a Hellenic dream. Her movements and the sculptured folds of her draperies seemed like the awakening to life of a marble frieze, in perfect harmony with Gluck's music. She often quoted a letter of Calzabigi, Gluck's librettist, in which he spoke of 'the essentially dramatic nature of the recitatives', which demanded a 'pitiless articulation and pauses instinct with life'. She made the audience feel that they were sharing her interpretation, and she herself drew strength from their response.

Pierre de Bréville asked her to create the leading rôle in his opera *Eros vainqueur*, a rôle that showed an entirely new side of her gifts, and in which her wit, gaiety and delicious irony found full scope. Then, in 1913, came Vincent d'Indy's revival in Paris of Monteverdi's *The Coronation of Poppea* in which she sang Poppea, and an opera by André Cardinal Destouches. At the Monnaie that winter, she sang Pénélope in the first performance in Belgium of Fauré's opera of that name — one of her most noble and beautiful interpretations. Especially notable, it was said, was her 'restraint, her royal simplicity of gesture, and psychological understanding — making an interpretation that was both Greek and modern'.

During these years she became the friend and chosen interpreter of Duparc, Fauré, d'Indy, Bréville, and of Debussy with whom of all musicians she had the greatest musical affinities. She loved to quote his definition of French musical genius: 'La fantaisie dans la sensibilité.' The first time he heard her sing his songs he said: 'What a joy to hear my songs sung as I have written them!' And shortly afterwards he asked her at very short notice to sing a whole series of his works in which he accompanied her. Later, in her talks, she emphasized Debussy's horror of noise . . . everything must be 'nuances de la sonorité', as he attached far more importance to the colour and quality of a sound than to its quantity — which he rather mistrusted. In his songs he imposed the exact musical rhythm that the words of the poem demanded.

In 1914 the Opéra-Comique claimed her to sing *Werther* and *Orpheus*, and, as a result of her beautiful creation of the rôle in Brussels, engaged her to give the first performance in Paris of Fauré's *Pénélope*, but the outbreak of war interrupted the rehearsals and put a stop to the productions. During the First World War Claire Croiza gave her services without stint. She sang with the Théâtre des Armées at la Panne—that free corner of Belgium where Queen Elisabeth of the Belgians organized concerts for the troops and the wounded. She sang at Nieuport and near the front, where she met the famous Dr Depage and the eminent painter Bastien, who became her lasting friends, and she shared further concerts with Ysaÿe. She sang in Geneva and in Italy for the Red Cross, and for her work she was awarded the Order of Leopold, being the first woman artist to receive this decoration from King Albert. There is no doubt that her experiences in these years, and the scenes she witnessed, gave her a deep and lasting conviction that war was the greatest evil that could befall mankind. She could not bear to witness suffering or hear tales of cruelty. She was very quick to defend others, but often refused to defend herself.

Subsequently, in Paris she sang the first stage version of Debussy's *Blessed Damoiselle* (*La demoiselle élue*) and took part in many of his works including the *Martyrdom of St Sebastian*. She often sang with André Caplet, and never tired of saying how much she owed to his peerless musicianship. Later, she created his *Mirror of Jesus*, and this lovely work is dedicated to her. At this time she branched out in two new directions: Jacques Copeau asked her to give recitals of music and poetry based on the poems of Verlaine and the Romantics, and M. Mangeot persuaded her to give her first public classes at the Ecole Normale de Musique in Paris. Besides Copeau, the poet Valéry recognized her poetic gifts, and when, in 1925, a dinner was given in her honour by Roussel, Grovlez, Bréville, Schmitt, Honegger and other leading musicians and writers of the day, which Valéry was unable to attend, he wrote her a letter—to be read at the dinner — which was afterwards published. In it, Valéry said:

A long time ago the idea came to me of enticing a singer to poetry. Here is how it came to me, and from what processes of thought.

Poetry is not music: still less is it speech. It is perhaps this ambiguity which gives it its refinement. One can say that it is about to sing, rather than that it sings: that it is about to explain itself rather than that it explains itself. It dares neither to sound forth too loudly, nor to speak too distinctly. It haunts neither the peaks nor the abysses of the voice. It is content with its hills, and with a very moderate profile. Yet by doing what it may with rhythm, stresses and consonants, it attempts to convey an almost musical quality to the expression of certain thoughts. Not of all thoughts.

Normal diction begins from prose and raises itself up to verse. It often happens that the sound of its drama, or the flow of its eloquence is confused with the intrinsic musicality of language. In that case the interpreter gains in effects what the poem loses in harmony. But I wished to try with a voice which, on the contrary, descended from the full and complete melody of musicians to our poets' melody, which is restrained and temperate. I had dreamed of . . . a voice which was assured throughout its range, a skilful voice, alive, far more aware, more crisp in its attack, more rich in its sonorities, more attentive to the tempi and to the silences, more marked in the changes of tone, than are the voices which are generally employed in speaking works in verse.

This idea encountered you; or rather the idea seemed to merge itself in your form, dear Croiza.

When I said to you: You sing and I am delighted! Now then, dare! . . .

At once you showed me a face in which fear and enthusiasm were united in one great desire. Your look seemed to say to poetry: 'You would not have found me, had I not already sought you out.'

Do you remember our experiments? With Ronsard open in front of us; the works of this Ronsard, who hummed his verses as he accompanied himself on the lute, these works served us as the subject of our researches. . . .

Our studies did not take long. Never have I seen a more prompt understanding of the musical system of poetry. Your soul, dear and noble artist, possessed it in all its power. I salute you and I admire you. The purest fire is in you!

Her speaking voice was beautiful, low and vibrant, and like her exquisite singing, a voice one wished to recall, whose echoes haunted the ear, that one never forgot.

During the 1930s, she gave a series of recitals that amply fulfilled the title 'An Anthology of French Music'. She never ceased adding to her repertoire, for she served her contemporaries and the young composers as ardently as those already established. At Fauré's death in 1924 she sang his *Pénélope* at the Opéra-Comique under the direction of Désiré Emile Inghelbrecht, and at La Petite Scène Monteverdi's Penelope in his opera *The Return of Ulysses*. The same year she came to London and gave three recitals, besides singing at some of the brilliant music parties of the season. Shortly afterwards she created the *Judith* of Honegger in Switzerland and he dedicated this work to her. Two years later came the first performance at Antwerp under de Vocht of *Les Choéphores*, a poem of Claudel set to music by Darius Milhaud, in which Croiza gave the wonderful 'exhortation'.

In January 1928 she came to London again, after an absence of four years, to sing for one of Gerald Cooper's concerts, and for the Kensington Music Club, and if I now speak of my own experience, it is because I believe it to be typical of the help she gave to many other singers at various stages of their studies and careers. It was the first time I had heard her sing. It amused her afterwards to know that, owing to a fortunate muddle over the tickets, I was placed near the front in a row bearing a placard 'Reserved for deaf members'! This recital was typical of many she gave subsequently in this country, and to several of her listeners it was a landmark in their musical lives.

This moving tragedienne and accomplished actress was simplicity itself on the concert platform. She exercised a complete ascendency over her audience and was herself extremely sensitive to what she called 'l'acoustique humaine de la salle'. Entering quietly and rather gravely, she acknowledged our greeting very charmingly, and then, absolutely still, but with the most expressive face and voice, she sang first some airs of Lully and Purcell. The atmosphere of the rather grim hall was transformed; time and place moved back into another world. Her technique was so accomplished that one was hardly aware of it. Then, in complete contrast, followed a group of traditional airs, full of life, wit and charm. The programme ended with songs by Fauré, Duparc, Roussel, Caplet and Debussy, and, as the *Daily Telegraph* wrote at the time, 'She sang these songs so that one felt they sprang so from the composer's brain, a miracle of interpretation with no apparent effort.' She enchanted her audience by the variety and *fantaisie* (imagination and variety) of her interpretations, passing from the insouciance of Roussel's 'A un jeune gentilhomme' and the wit and 'scene of Italian Comedy', as she called it, of Debussy's setting of Verlaine's 'Fantoches', to the depth of feeling in the same composer's 'Recueillement', 'Harmonie du soir' and 'Le Jet d'eau' — all three with poems by Baudelaire. And the revelation of her warm humanity and generous heart (qualities not always allied to a brilliant intelligence) made her singing of Fauré's 'Prison' an unforgettably moving experience. We had, in fact, heard one who in France was called 'the ideal interpreter of pure music, of the musical sensibility of our time'. After the concert, Mrs Norman O'Neill introduced me to Mme Croiza, who, before I could thank her, characteristically said: 'Ah! it was you who were sitting just in front. Thank you for all your sympathy. What a difference it makes to see a happy, responsive face that shares one's own emotion!' and on Mrs O'Neill's saying she wished she would hear me sing while she was in London, Croiza kindly consented.

My friend Esther Fisher came with me and delighted Croiza by her playing. I had already given my first recital, but felt I had come to an impasse and was making no interpretative progress. Croiza at once put her finger on the cause. She asked if I wished for a really candid opinion and, after congratulating me on what was good, she said 'When you were listening to me your expression changed all the time, but when you sing, your voice is expressive but not your face. It is a question of courage and self-confidence. One day one says to oneself "whatever it costs me I will try to give this or that nuance of expression", and when you see how the public responds to it you dare to express yourself still further.' She then proceeded to analyse the Chausson and Gluck which I had taken to sing — a royal present, indeed, for a friendly audition!

Subsequently I was privileged to enjoy many lessons and classes. I wish I could convey the inspiration of those lessons and of the new horizons they opened. Claire Croiza was infinitely kind to her pupils. Her charming flat in Paris mirrored her personality and her taste . . . no overcrowding; a few good pictures; and photographs, including ones of Debussy, Baudelaire, Mary Garden and Eleanora Duse. There were shelves and shelves of books, and music manuscripts, many of which had been given her by the composers.

Technically, she was never dogmatic. She had sung, listened and read so continuously and widely that she liked to assemble and compare the points of voice-production on which the great teachers of the past and the throat specialists of the day were in agreement. She would stress the danger to young singers of forcing beyond their natural limitations; and advised them 'to learn to distinguish between what you like to do, and what you are able to do'. She would urge them to find their own 'personal rhythm' and to adapt their individual physique to the basic principles of *bel canto*. But she would quote the singer who told her that her voice had been damaged by a self-styled exponent of the Garcia method, and restored by another teacher who also taught the Garcia method. She spoke of the effect that language must have on emission, of the

ideal phonetics of Italian, the danger of faulty nasal predomin-
ance in French, or mistaken throaty placement in German, of
the possible disadvantages of the many consonants and
equivocal vowels in English. 'Chanter claire et sonore', she
would repeat. 'Work at scales — the source of vocal articulation
— at vocalises, exercises, and the old Italian repertoire until you
achieve that "homogénéité de la série sonore" and free yourself
from the obsession of tone-in-the-singular that so often
prevents the singer from concentrating on the music he is
singing. Work at variety of timbre, use your palette of sound as
a painter uses his palette.'

Musically, she insisted on a scrupulous exactitude in
following the composer's indications of notation and rhythm,
and on impeccable intonation (one of her attributes). 'You must
separate and not confuse "movement, expression, nuance",'
she said. 'Try to phrase like an instrumentalist, to achieve purity
of line and the curve and dynamics of the musical phrase; know
how to begin and how to end, and give due deference to the
planes of the composition. You must attain the physical
relaxation necessary to free your intelligence.'

Croiza would speak of the tragedy for the singer in being
both the instrument and instrumentalist, but stress his
privilege in having two masters to serve — the musician and
the poet. 'Soak yourself in the music as a whole,' she said.
'Work at the melody until you are part of it, and then repeat
the words a hundred times over out loud. Study the poem
away from the music, so that you know what the words really
mean.' She would demonstrate all that can be meant by that
composite word 'diction', with her own infinitely varied
articulation — varied according to the demands of tragedy,
comedy, lyric poetry or operetta. She spoke of the 'volupté du
son', of the pure pronunciation of vowels; of the consonants
stressed in relation to the meaning and feeling of the context;
and of the 'accent that gives life to the phrase'. Her subtle
colouring and nuance was an example that filled the student
with exaltation and despair but certainly stimulated the
exercising of lazy tongue and flabby lips!

When speaking of interpretation she would stress the need for 'forgetfulness of self' and say: 'Try to eliminate the self-torment that prevents the singer from identifying himself with his "personnage". Try to free that "other self" so that we are completely absorbed by the music, the poem, the beauty of the whole. We must have the courage to bare our soul, to express our faith and enthusiasm; we must create and live the characters in a scene of our imagining, and the face as well as the voice must, through our inward conviction and concentration, allow the actor to take precedence over the singer. In order to have something to express, we must interest ourselves in many things, awaken the mind, stimulate the imagination, escape from our everyday self, renew ourselves constantly. Talent alone is not enough, it must be enriched by our own inward enrichment; no one can be a great artist who has not gaiety and variety as well as dramatic power. Never miss an opportunity of seeing or hearing a beautiful work, a fine artist, a great performance, and when listening try to benefit yourself instead of criticizing in a carping, prejudiced, stupid manner!' Croiza always spoke as an artist, she never pontificated.

At her London classes she was handicapped by the language. She must have suffered from the mangling of her beloved poets, but she never let it appear. More like a charming hostess than a teacher, she tried to put the executants at their ease, allowing herself only a little caressing irony at times. In cases of conceit, of mannerisms and grimaces, or if she felt a real talent was taking a wrong road, she could be uncompromisingly frank (she said there ought to be a 'class of discouragement' for those who should not take up singing as a career), but no one sincerely wishing for advice asked in vain.

In Paris, where the majority of her audiences were French, her eloquence took wing, and she expressed herself with such rare virtuosity and enthusiasm for the music, or a good performance, that even the most nervous executant felt a sympathetic partnership with the listeners. The subjects of these classes were manifold. I have noted over 45 in my notebooks and programmes, ranging from such general subjects as Respect for Music, Repertoire, Psychology, Imagination and Nationality in Interpretation, the Expressive Value of Words, What Musicians Have Said about Singers, Careers of Yesterday and To-day, etc., to more specialized talks on different periods of music and individual composers and songs. Hélène Abraham's notes, which she took down verbatim, are of inestimable value to students and lovers of French music, of music in general and singing in particular. Indeed, much of Croiza's teaching has been preserved by the author of that book.

From 1928 onwards, and until her class at the Paris Conservatoire made it impossible, Croiza visited England four or five times a year. She gave recitals, and she sang for Anthony Bernard's concerts and festivals of French music, for the Institut Français, and for many music clubs in London and the provinces. She gave many broadcasts, her programmes representing the whole field of French song writers from Lully to Debussy, Roussel, Caplet and Honegger, in which she loved to be accompanied by Ernest Lush. Croiza was really only happy singing in her own incomparable tongue, but on one occasion André Mangeot asked us both to sing at the St John Music Club, and to include two or three duets of Purcell. It was, of course, a great privilege for me and, as a compliment, Croiza made a great and conscientious effort to master our rebellious English pronunciation, but in 'Sound the Trumpet' the hard s, th, tr, somehow became involved and a disastrous *fou-rire* was narrowly avoided! She became very fond of her London audiences, and sang many songs which were then still unfamiliar to the English public, for example, those of Roussel.

Her London visits had to be fitted in between heavy commitments on the continent, but she made time to visit the National Gallery, the Tate Gallery and the British Museum, and to go to any outstanding concert, opera, or film. I shall always remember her joy at hearing Rosa Ponselle in *La Traviata* at Covent Garden, and at hearing Toscanini conduct.

She loved English comedians and never missed a chance of seeing Cicely Courtneidge, whom she took off to perfection in her scene of an English governess mistaking absinth for tea in a bar at Ostend. She delighted in strolling through Harrods, or visiting Woolworths in Oxford Street to find the newest 'Dinky' for her son. Being human, she had her foibles, and one was letter-writing. She would bring a suitcase of unanswered letters to England with her, and would say virtuously: 'This evening we will stay in the hotel and tackle my correspondence'; but hardly was the first letter triumphantly achieved when some chance reference to a book, performance, musician, actor or topic of interest would let loose a spellbinding flood of conjecture, discussion or memories, and the letters would go back in the suitcase for another occasion.

As her time for lessons in London was so limited, Mme Croiza held a series of holiday summer classes. The first one was at Caux, overlooking the Lake of Geneva, where we all enjoyed the magnificent scenery. In her teaching — whenever the poem invoked nature — she would urge the pupil to imagine some such countryside, in the place of the somewhat suburban landscapes they sometimes appeared to visualize. Another summer we went to Zoute, and it was a revelation to visit Bruges with her, and to be privileged to enjoy her wide culture and love and knowledge of beautiful and historical places. There, she showed us the Béguinage, that haven for the old, where the nuns give the inmates the rest and — if they wish it — the solitude that Croiza herself would have appreciated in her life of ceaseless activity.

The following year a beloved friend, Mrs Crombie, took a charming house at Swanage where there was room for us, for the lessons, and for her own family, which included six grandchildren. Croiza really enjoyed this slice of English family life, and the companionship of our charming hostess in the calm of her well-ordered household. On this occasion, and in the previous summers, Croiza was accompanied by one of her oldest friends, Ivana Meedintiano, a veritable torrent of music and conversation. She played for the lessons and coached us in between. She had lived all her life amongst musicians and had a marvellous musical instinct. When she had a villa at Monte Carlo she helped many artists with unparallelled generosity. Croiza used to relate that if — for the sake of economy — Ivana took a tram, on alighting she would run to the front to tip the driver. They would reminisce delightfully about concerts and tours.

One of the loveliest summers was spent at Bréthencourt, at the country house in the wide plain of La Beauce which belonged to Croiza and her sister, and from which we made two unforgettable expeditions to Chartres — on bicycles. Here, in the midst of her family she was happy and content, and would gladly have spent more time had the ceaseless demands of her profession and her financial burdens allowed it. She worshipped in the old village church.

The last summer that was undisturbed by rumours of war we spent at Houlgate in Brittany where my husband and I became engaged, and I shall never forget her kindness to us. In 1938 and 1939 she came to our home in Buckinghamshire, but on each occasion the course was interrupted, first by the threat and then by the outbreak of war. We begged her to remain with us, but she felt she must return to her own home and to her class at the Conservatoire. The privations of war — she lost over four stone in weight — and the mental anguish she suffered undoubtedly caused the fatal illness that overtook her in 1946. She died on 27 May that year.

During the years when she came so frequently to England, her concerts and classes in Paris and at the Conservatoires of Paris, Geneva and Brussels, the congresses at which she spoke, and the juries on which she adjudicated and the festivals of Duparc, Fauré, Debussy, Caplet, Roussel and Ravel at which she sang, make up a sum of achievement that is both admirable and astonishing. In 1931 she was made a Chevalier de la Légion d'honneur for her services to French music. Of her French pupils, Janine Micheau, Suzanne Juyol, Camille Maurane, Gérard Souzay, Jacques Jansen, and many others bear testimony to her teaching; whilst the number of pupils from all over Europe and even from India and Japan is impossible to assess. However tired Claire Croiza might be before a concert, a conference or a class, she would enter at once into the 'skin' of her subject or music. The mercury would begin to rise, and her inward fire and radiance shone through until she was the embodiment of intense life. 'Vis avec force', she would urge her pupils.

Claire Croiza was a beautiful exponent of religious music. Her faith was at the centre of her being, and the well from which she drew her strength and quiet courage, her gallant acceptance of whatever life brought her. She was so intensely vital, so fully aware of beauty in all its manifestations that others lived more completely when in her company. She is remembered for all her sparkling gifts, her supreme intelligence, but above all for her deep humanity, her kindness and the simple nobility and spirituality of her presence.

Subsequent chapters of this book are condensed from the verbatim reports of Croiza's classes and, within the limits of translation, appear as nearly as possible in her own words, except that editorial interpolations appear within square brackets.

B. B.

Claire Croiza's Classes

PART I
Performing

ONE

HOW TO WORK AT SINGING

THE VOICE IS the most beautiful of all instruments because it is human. The voice is the instrument of the music, and the word is the instrument of the thought.

The singer has the sublime privilege of uniting music and poetry. The quality of the voice is the most precious element in singing. But singing is not only a voice, not only articulation, it is a total of many elements difficult to enumerate and to define. If the first quality of the singer resides in the natural timbre of his voice, the sensitiveness with which, like an instrumentalist, he can play with the timbre and vary it, is the most precious element in singing. That is why this is not to be a course on the voice. Do not imagine that I am going to show you a larynx with a lot of learned and complicated explanations. That would be the same mistake that a professor of the dance would make if he spoke only about the fibula and the patella.

I would ask all singers to love the music more than they do and to be more conscientious in their work. In order to be understood it is not enough to explain. In singing, as in life, it is the sad truth that we never understand anything we have not discovered ourselves. As Voltaire said, 'One cannot have a correct idea of what one has not experienced'. I am not claiming to give you a 'key' to the art of singing. In fact, is there such a key? Every time I have heard great singers, I have tried to get them to speak about their method and of their art, and I have not found two who followed the same method.

There is only one thing that counts in art, and that is the final result. It is of little importance how we get there, so long as we do achieve our aim. All methods employed are legitimate in our work, provided they do not show in the final result. In all work, what counts is to find our own personal rhythm. The best teacher is the one who helps you to find your own rhythm. The work of a teacher must be a form of research by two people, undertaken with mutual confidence. I do not like the word 'teacher'. In our work there are two people; one searches and the other guides. The great singer is the one who has found the key to his personal system: and, of course, there are no two key-holes alike — because they are human. The advice given to a pupil is a kind of 'sowing of seeds' in his mind. The result of this sowing does not always show at once; the seed may not ripen until much later, but the important thing is that the student must be a soil.

We must be a soil for all the seeds that come to us either by nature or by art. Our own powers cannot be enough to nourish our interpretations, we must enrich ourselves: we must discover life instead of ignoring it, and force ourselves to understand, to love, to know. It is easier to put the brake on a powerful car than to make a donkey walk at 100 miles per hour. We must not be afraid of loving our music too much, nor of varying and renewing our repertoire.

We must try and understand the reason for the faults of others. When I listen I am always working. If someone asks me, 'With whom did you work?' I could answer, 'With all the singers I have heard'.

The tragedy of the singer is that he is at the same time the instrument and the instrumentalist, and too often in singing the instrument is sacrificed to the instrumentalist, or the player to the instrument. Rare indeed are the singers who have known how to make the most of both sides of their art and to develop each to the same point of perfection. The voice is the most beautiful of instruments but also the most fragile. A pianist or violinist can choose a perfect instrument and have it repaired if it is damaged, but the singer has no choice. He must make do with the instrument he has been given: it is for him to keep it in good condition and to perfect it—his own instrument does not resemble any other. At the beginning of his studies, he must do detailed work on this instrument; the component parts must be verified one by one before making use of the 'motor', and not set up hastily without preliminary work. Too many singers remain attached to the sound — ['son'] in the singular which is still more serious.

It is 'le regard' — the glance — by which, above all, the face becomes alive. The two most beautiful 'regards' that I have seen on the stage are those of Rose Caron and of Mary Garden. When we sing something addressed to someone, we must place it at eye level — not in the sky. Unless he is speaking of trees or of birds a singer on stage must have only one look, directed to the interlocutor's face. He must take a 'point de repère' [a guiding mark] and there place the person whom he is addressing, or the scene or the object he is looking at. In the same way I must recommend all singers not to position their stage characters — even when they are dead — in the sky; do not hold a conversation with people in the gallery of the theatre. It is not possible. These are details the public does not realize exactly because its power of analysis is not sufficiently developed, but it is difficult to exaggerate how much a singer can make the words he pronounces live by his look. If the exact personality of the composer and the poet is alive in us, everything will fall into place without our willing it, for we are living the poem, the story, the recitative or the tragedy that we should be seeing in front of us as we pronounce the words.

It sometimes happens that one may achieve what one can do, but one never achieves what one wishes to do. Our performances always fall short of our ideals. But we must be sufficiently penetrated by the text and the music to be quite sure of what we want to do. In interpretation one of the most difficult things is to sustain vitality: there must be no drop in expression, no 'air pockets'; but do not confuse vitality and expressiveness with agitation. Our starting point must be in relaxation.

We must achieve relaxation in singing. One of the advantages of the opera house over the concert hall is that, there, the singer is obliged to think of several things at the same time.

The demands of the producer for his place on the stage, the conductor for the tempo; and the multiplicity of these demands, liberates the singer from his singing, preventing him from being absorbed by the voice. Many concert arias would gain by being practised while doing something else: either sewing or sorting a work-basket or something of the kind. They would gain in naturalness, in suppleness, in life. I was always told how the second Madame Debussy sang as she arranged a vase of flowers, and carried on her everyday life with absolute naturalness. Well — it is this we should achieve, but with modern songs to achieve such an interior independence needs an enormous amount of work.

Once the voice is well placed, it is legitimate to pay attention to the shape of the mouth (in a mirror) while singing, to think of our singer's voice when we practise: it is even a virtue, provided it be done at home — on the platform we must not think of it any more, pay no more attention to it, but let ourselves sing relaxedly, with a natural mouth, and a natural face — not with a singer's face and a singer's mouth. The life of our facial expression is in the eyes and in the mouth: the mouth that speaks, the mouth that sings, the mouth that lives, and not the mouth of a singer deformed by the emission of the sound, nor a lifeless mouth that kills the facial expression — in fact a natural mouth in a natural face.

The singer must beware of any movement of the head or of the body in singing. His body should not exist, should not move; it must never attract attention. Everything must be concentrated on the face as if it came out from behind a curtain; and on this face, the windows of the mouth and of the eyes should be particularly expressive. Never sing leaning forward, sing with the shoulders held back. As soon as the listener's attention is caught by the singer's body, his dress etc., it leaves the music. Not only must he not move, but everything should happen at head-level, only on the face! A bodily immobility combined with a lively facial expression. Avoid the habit of clenching the hands; no one may notice it but you will contract yourself. Sing with relaxed arms.

Ideally, before singing, do some exercises with supple arms to improve relaxation. Singers, I believe, do not do enough exercises to promote suppleness. They do not need the athletic work of the dancer, but they do need to discover the natural balance of the body, and, for the theatre, of their gestures. There is a distinction between natural suppleness and trained suppleness. Singers must not be satisfied with a natural suppleness, they must work to acquire a trained suppleness. If a horse were to contract when he jumped a fence, he would hit it. Similarly, the singer must aim at total equilibrium of his body. How often he stiffens up and thereby makes difficulties for himself; he becomes like the jockey who spurs on his horse and pulls the bit in every direction, whereas the good jockey is one whom the horse does not feel but whom he obeys; contraction is a major enemy of the interpreter.

Nobility and simplicity are the most beautiful qualities in a performance, but they do not exclude sensibility. One must not be noble and severe, but noble and alive. We express gaiety, we express suffering, but we rarely express deep happiness, though this is at the base of many song-texts. We look only for sadness and when we are full of happiness we become excited. Real, tranquil joy should not be agitated, irritated or over-excited. Rare indeed are the interpreters who, when singing a love poem, suggest or communicate the idea of quiet happiness, of that true happiness, one could say the happiness which half the human race runs after, the happiness which, through music, is within our reach every time we sing. I have often asked myself why, in singing, women often look sad and men furious? We must beware of force destroying the expression of our singing, of strength becoming rage; and even a tone of total intensity must still be loving, and not turn into anger. The singer may pass from one extreme to the other, or he may fail to make up his mind and remain in an unrelieved greyness — in eternal half-mourning. No, if he wishes to choose black or pink, he must also have all the intermediary colours of the spectrum at his disposal. Do not let us remain tepid — let joy and sadness have their colour —

do not give an uncommitted interpretation that has not taken sides, or an indefinite, 'n'ait pas pris parti' character; in interpretation it is better to make a mistake by over-affirmation than remain undecided. Make a mistake — but give me something alive, something that really exists.

One of the pitfalls for the singer is the fear of ridicule. We are afraid of looking foolish, but we must at all costs give something, and sing with life. Operetta is a wonderful exercise in exteriorization because it is full of imagination and as animated as life itself. The longer I live, the more I admire music-hall singers who sing with their bodies and faces naturally, instead of like us, with our helmets and cuirasses; we must dare to exteriorize.

What is needed to sing? To have a voice, musical sensibility, and to work at this voice.

Singing, as I have said a thousand times, is the sublime union of music and poetry. The singer is obliged to think about the music, but in fact very often he pays attention only to the sound, or the succession of sounds. But that is still only the voice, it is not 'song' or 'singing' since 'song' also comprises a text, a poem that must be pronounced and understood.

I find that so many singers begin to sing before having a well-established 'key-board', this homogeneity of the sonorous scale. It is for the singer to make himself an established vocal plan, a firm vocalization, a firm vocal articulation. Just now I listened to Mlle Meedintiano playing trills in an accompaniment, and I said to myself, 'Ah! here is instrumental vocalization!' But few singers can do that with their voices. [In a later talk Mme Croiza instanced Rosa Ponselle's wonderful vocalization.] Therefore, technique — 'not more than five minutes at a time,' says Garcia; 'not more than half-an-hour on end,' says a great Viennese doctor — but as many five-minutes, or also as many half-hours as we can; a little at a time — but often — when we can concentrate on certain musical phrases, work at them for months on end if we wish, as the virtuosi do.

There is therefore the voice, there is also the music, and there is this wonderful *solfège* (the terror of singers), without which it is impossible to acquire exactness and rhythm. Rhythm! We only have to hear the treatment to which the unfortunate Chopin is made to submit! How many pianists play exactly? It is not only the singer who may not be musician enough. To be a musician is something apart from the voice, apart from virtuosity, apart from everything else.

The singer has all my indulgence because he begins to learn music too late. A young pianist begins his training very early. But a singer, No. With most of us, childhood is not directed towards music, which does not come unconsciously but must be acquired by work. And when it comes too late, it fatally resembles a 'nouveau-riche'.

But these questions are not to be decided or condemned brutally — let us try to understand first the 'why' of things. In old times singers only worked on 'Ah'. Nowadays, so many different kinds of 'Ah' have been distinguished there is no general agreement about it, and we begin to vocalize on all the other vowels in order to arrive finally at the (Italian) 'a'. Another point — the kind of voice: 'Am I a mezzo, a soprano? am I a tenor, a baritone?' Voices change. Bonnier says in his book: 'Jean de Reszke first sang all the baritone roles before becoming a tenor'. In the same way Mario, another famous tenor, had been a baritone and Mongini, a tenor who gave the high 'D' easily, had debuted as a bass. Lhérie (the first Don José in *Carmen*) had also been a baritone before becoming a tenor. And amongst women errors of classification are no less frequent. Many sopranos and altos have destroyed their voices in wishing too soon to be the 'falcons' they would perhaps have become naturally a few years later. [Marie Cornélie Falcon (1814–1897) was a French singer with a unique voice of exceptional range.]

Do not let us seek too much, especially with our modern repertoire, to develop too heavy a voice. Everyone knows that there is one thing above all others that matters, and that is the quality of the voice. When the body of the double-bass is missing, the strings will never give the sonority of a double-bass, and in our human construction, our nature must not be forced. At the outset let us use the voice on which we can work with facility. Do not let us concentrate on that which is bad; otherwise we get irritated and we do not achieve anything.

The timbre of the voice should always be 'clear and sonorous', and not confused with 'clear and white'. Naturally, it is not a question of always singing 'clear' or always 'dark'; singing demands the two, but in working, practise 'clear and sonorous', as the old Italians did.

Stéphen de la Madelaine said: 'Any voice that does not know how to rest in the cantabile on the clear Timbre, and that does not "nuance" its effects, frays itself, and disappears after a certain time.'

For articulation, I think it should be the same in singing as in speaking: energetic, but not redoubled, and applied according to the meaning of the words [see chapter three].

Another most serious error is to work at everything with the voice, singing loud, even shouting. All should be worked in parallel, but separately, and never too loud, never! The voice must be treated homoeopathically, especially the female voice.

I do not want to dwell too much on 'Expression' today, and prolong this talk; but what women especially should understand, is that to arrive at being able to express, it is essential to take an interest in many things, to understand many things, and to put our intelligence to work to the same extent as our 'sound system'. The most beautiful voice that is capable only of giving out sounds without expressing anything else, without knowing how to utilize itself, or make the most of itself, is not interesting.

In general, I find that the singer who is starting a career is not sufficiently in love with the quality and the colours of his or her voice. The repertoire, the size of the halls, incite him to seek above all the piercing effect. For our foundation we must work at scales, vocalises and exercises like any instrumentalist, and begin on the old Italian repertoire of light arias, lighter than our voice, and never at arias lower than our natural tessitura. And in Gluck we have a musician superior to all others for the work of declamation and pronunciation, for Gluck's arias and recitatives are for the singer as Chopin is for the pianist.

TWO

RESPECT FOR THE MUSICAL TEXT

THE INTERPRETER IS for the composer what light is for the painter.

The voice is an instrument that causes the instrumentalist before and during performance constant preoccupations. Art, on the contrary, demands complete freedom, and to find a balance between this freedom and this preoccupation is one of the difficulties of the singer's task. If he is incapable, while singing, of listening to the music at least as much as to his own voice, he will never make an interpreter. Absolute musical accuracy is rare — as recordings prove. A singer's first duty is to sing the music as it is written and to give to every note the value that the composer has given it. The note, the syllable, the word must be in place before attempting so-called interpretation. This is easier in modern music than in that of the past, because today composers indicate everything they want. If singers were faithful to the notation, to the actual *solfège*, they would sing much better.

I am often astonished at the fact that singers and instrumentalists in general — for we are instrumentalists, too — have so little respect for the music as written by the composer. At the beginning of our practising we do not take enough trouble to find out the rhythm desired by the composer, or to observe the care he has taken over the value of a note, or a rest, which may be infinitesimal. When one thinks of the hours, of the nights of hesitation and work spent by the composer, one is dumbfounded at the interpreter's lack of respect. We do not work with enough love — life gets in the way. Everyone is in a hurry. The rehearsal must finish at the appointed time, the conductor neglects a detail, the instrumentalist does not notice it, or lets it pass. The value of each note should be looked at with a magnifying glass. Perhaps it is because the precise composers of today mistrust the possible bad taste of some interpreters, that they note everything to the least detail. They indicate everything that should be done and the interpreter has nothing to add, nothing to modify. His magnificent rôle is to serve and not to collaborate.

Think of Debussy's remark that Caplet liked to quote. Someone recommended a singer, assuring Debussy that in her he would have a real collaborator, and Debussy replied, 'An interpreter will be enough for me'. In general the instrumental side does not interest the singer. He certainly needs an ally in music, but once he has a beautiful instrument, he thinks only of that and too often forgets to be an instrumentalist. It is an everlasting conflict and composers have always reproached singers with it. In the words of Berlioz:

> I have already said, a singer capable of singing only sixteen bars of good music, with a natural voice, well-placed, sympathetic, and able to sing them without effort, without breaking up the phrase, without exaggerating the accents to a violent degree, without faults in the French, without dangerous liaisons, without platitude, without affectation, without hiatus, without insolent modifications of the text, without transpositions, without faulty intonation, without a limping rhythm, without ridiculous ornaments or nauseating appoggiaturas, finally in such a way that the composer's period becomes understandable and remains quite simply what he has written, is a rare bird, very rare, excessively rare.

I think, in spite of Berlioz' exaggeration, that this is the feeling of all composers. In a general way they complain, often with justice, in fact, of singers paying too much attention to their voices, and not enough to their art.

Singers, like all interpreters of music, must respect, without confusion: rhythm and tempo; tempo and nuance; nuance and expression. 'Rhythm,' says Alain, 'is the division of the time by the different intensities that recur in a certain order. Movement [tempo] is the degree of quickness or of slowness. The tempo of a symphony may be arguable, its rhythm never. Nuance is the degree of softness or of power, the decrease or increase of sonority.' La Argentina diminishes or augments the sonority of her castanets without slowing up or quickening the tempo. Expression is the quality of emotion contained in the work transmitted by the sensibility of the interpreter. The nuances of the music do not always coincide with the nuances of expression. Expression can be intensified with a sound that diminishes. An example is the end of Fauré's 'Soir' — 'Tes yeux levés au ciel si tristes et si doux.' [See comments on songs in chapter eight].

I listened recently to Debussy's third ballad, 'Les Femmes de Paris', and heard a *rallentando* where I knew there should be an *animato*; the singer was a good one, but after she had finished singing I looked at her copy of the song and saw that someone had crossed out Debussy's *animato* and written *rallentando*! I am astonished to find gramophone recordings that contain formidable infidelities of tempo and rhythm . . . for there must have been an instrumentalist, a conductor and a sound-engineer to commit them, and to let them pass. It is not once but ten times that one experiences this shock at hearing a work deformed in such a way. There is also often a difference between the composer's tempo and the conductor's tempo, and even a difference in the composer's tempo if one works with him twice. But there is one thing that does not change and that is the rhythm.

I find it altogether too much when music is not served with respect — it gives me a kind of interrupted heart beat. The singer comes on to the platform as the mouthpiece of the composer and the poet, and must respect the tempo, respect everything. A change of tempo can kill a work. It is impossible to sing 'in time' enough. Musically everything must be rigorously exact, be sung with metronomic precision, and the same is true whether of Debussy or of Duparc. Duparc once said to me, 'If I had known how much some interpreters exaggerate *rallentandi*, I would never have dared to indicate them.'

Respect modifications of tempo without amplifying them, and above all do not confuse tempo and nuance — the one has nothing to do with the other. Never make a *rallentando* on a *pianissimo* or hurry a *crescendo* when only a change of nuance is indicated. The singer must find his expression within the framework of the tempo and the rhythm: we must work on a foundation of precision. To add nothing, to deform nothing, to keep strictly to what is written, to stay within the framework and the rhythm that the composer has created, is an inflexible rule.

I ask it as a favour: music should be approached with love, and one should not change anything in it. However, our task is easy if we are faithful to what is written. When we compare the singer and the actor, we see how much easier it is for us to interpret: everything is given us, we have only to obey, while the actor must find his own rhythm and everything else as well. Intonation is worked at by the singer because he wants to sing in tune, but he never pays enough attention to rhythm, which is the backbone of music, and there is never enough backbone in what we hear. Those with whom we work are never sufficiently particular. Happy are they who encounter conductors who are hard to please! Above all, in opera, faults in a great number of rôles are neglected and they become habitual by repetition, they establish themselves and are transmitted, so that a false tradition is established.

Above, and before all else, is the music. *Solfège* may be the terror of singers but, without it, it is impossible to achieve precision and rhythm. A singer who cannot read music easily gives me the same impression as an actor who cannot read. If we do not accustom ourselves very quickly to the exact note, to the exact sonority, our minds will never be free to interpret; we shall always be preoccupied by the musical side. The foundation of all this is *solfège*. I can bear bad singing but I cannot bear performances in which the tempo is demolished. Singers should be concerned with two points: intonation and rhythm — and it is not only singers who are insufficiently musicianly, the same is true of instrumentalists. To be a musician is to be something apart — apart from the voice, apart from knowledge, apart from virtuosity, apart from everything.

Music is not a question of knowing a great deal, it is a question of possessing an instinct for the phrase — something which cannot be acquired.

At the point I have reached in my life, and with the experience I have gained, I can say that anyone who sings may have beauty, knowledge and everything else, but if he has not an instinct for music as something to be served with his whole soul, he will never sing. A voice without phrasing does not exist. A phrase sung musically, even with very little voice, is in itself something admirable. Musical sensibility is everything, and all the lessons in the world will be of no use to someone who does not possess it. Those who are concerned with teaching, whether for their children or for themselves, should pay great attention to the difference between the gift and the pleasure. There should be a Class of Discouragement at the Conservatoire for those who have been misdirected! At the age of entry at the Conservatoire there is still time to step back, return to the cross-roads, and take another direction. Some teachers concentrate on vocal techniques — and they are right, we all work at that; but if they occupy themselves only with the vocal technique, they are wrong. If a pupil's voice 'loses' when he sings a rapid passage in the right tempo, they will make him slow it up. This is right for practising, but not in performance. If someone is incapable of singing at the right tempo, the only thing to do is not to sing in public. It is not music that should adjust itself to the performer. Music must come first, before everything else.

In the choice of tempi there is a 'sensibility of the moment' that is undeniable and exists even in the composers who do not always accompany in exactly the same way. But a semi-quaver always remains a quarter of a crotchet. It is simply a question of calculation. Faults of rhythm are unpardonable. In singing, music, dancing, nothing can be achieved without it.

The two indispensable qualities for the singer, apart from the voice, are good rhythm and good intonation. A soloist who sings out of tune is abominable but he destroys only himself; a singer in ensemble who lacks rhythm betrays not only the ensemble of the work and the composer, but also destroys the work of the others who sing with him. Practise rhythm apart from singing, everywhere — in the train, at the dentist — and make different rhythms fit into the same bar. With good rhythm and a good ear, a singer has little need of anything else, for singing remains above all a question of hearing. We too often forget the sensitiveness of the ear, without which a singer cannot do anything. If I could organize the teaching of singing according to my ideas, there would be a whole period devoted to the education of the ear. A true singer must acquire this quality; he must know how to listen.

We must contrive to free ourselves from all musical anxiety. When Toscanini rehearsed an orchestra he started by saying, 'Gentlemen, I am going to ask you for much patience. During an hour we are going to do nothing but *solfège.*' '*Mise en place*', a musical 'putting in place', is the starting point for every-thing, and every song presupposes an accord between voice and accompaniment. Their relationship to each other is as close as the dialogue in an acting rôle, especially in modern songs which are really sonatas for piano and voice. Singers must follow the impulsion given by the orchestra or the piano; listen to it, reply to it, and 'jump on to his horse in time'. Too often, when the voice enters, one has the impression that the gallant horse was keeping up his pace, and that all at once a weight of 1,000 kilos has been put into the carriage he was pulling.

Finally, we must beware of effects that succeed but have no meaning. In modern music, especially, a *pianissimo* must not be made without a reason, either for its own sake or for making a singer's pause aimed at effect. Nor should an excess of feeling ever give a note a greater value than it should be given. In Debussy's *Chansons de Bilitis*, at the last phrase but one of 'La Chevelure', if the composer had wanted a pause on the word 'tendre', he would certainly have indicated it; most singers, however, make one.

If we had within us a kind of exact graph of the music, and a good articulation, we should already have much talent, and not deform or disarrange anything. Debussy once said to me, 'If I had realized the formidable power of the interpreter, I think I should never have had the courage to compose.' No music passes directly from the composer to the listener; it must pass through the interpreter; if he betrays the composer the work is destroyed.

Among interpreters some serve themselves by means of the music, and some serve music itself. Let us serve music, renew our repertoires, and popularize the less well known compositions — the compositions of our own day. The most celebrated works gained their celebrity assuredly because they were beautiful, but there are others, less well known, that deserve to be performed. Let the interpreter be penetrated by the beauty of his rôle and be careful to respect the music, performing with precision and devotion, and serving the composers whose works could not live without him.

THREE

ARTICULATION AND PRONUNCIATION

ARTICULATION IS FOR the ear what the printed word is for the eye.

I do not reproach singers for concentrating on their voices, I reproach them for working only on the voice instead of lessening their vocal concern by developing in parallel within themselves the thought, the will, the expression. It is not enough to be satisfied with a beautiful voice; variety of expression must be added. Expression is not a question of intensity and force, but of understanding, of facial expression, of pronunciation. In singing one can give preference either to the sound or to the word. There are certain works where the vocal beauty must prevail, where the voice must crown the orchestra by its beauty of instrumental sound: for example, in the case of Wagner. But wherever the music does not demand it, you must give the importance due to articulation and pronunciation. In songs it is generally the pronunciation that should take the lead.

When we listen to singing, not when we listen with prejudice, but when we listen with generosity, with kindness, as we must listen in order to understand and learn something, it is amazing to find how few singers have reached the front rank in articulation. Still fewer among women singers, for men generally articulate better than women. For the majority of singers, the text unwinds itself in the memory like a kind of film that brings the words. But the idea, or the picture they express, escapes them. To interpret, an intimate assimilation of the text is necessary. The singer must understand the value given to the words by the composer and by the poet. He must

43

say them, and repeat them with firmness and clarity so that, passing from speaking the word to singing the text, he loses as little as possible of its carrying power and its 'accent'.

For the sense of the text must be understood by the listener, and in order that the sense be understood, the words must be easily heard. All authors are in agreement on the importance of articulation. It has been shown that there is a true physiological balance between the work of articulation and the work of the larynx, in such a way that if an effort is made with articulation, relief for the larynx is the result. Singing must not be left flabby, it must acquire muscle, and that is the rôle of articulation. The accent in singing is given by the attack of the consonants, but an energetic articulation of the consonants does not mean a brusque articulation. Good articulation must be searched for with suppleness. Learn to pronounce well, to pronounce in a noble way: know how to give more value to certain syllables that give the words their significance. It is never sufficiently realized what can be achieved in interpretation by the way in which a consonant is pronounced. From the point of view of expression everything is in the attack of the consonant. In Fauré's 'Soir', all the expression of the end, 'Tes yeux levés au ciel, si tristes et si doux', depends on the way we pronounce the consonant of this word, 'doux'. French has some consonants more 'explosive' than others, and use must be made of them in interpretation. The absence of the tonic accent in French must be supplemented by the accentuation of the consonants.

A beautiful articulation is coloured [varied]; its first importance is to colour a syllable. 'Amour' can be anguished, tender or satisfied. The difference lies in the way in which it is pronounced, and the manner in which the facial expression accompanies it. For the interpreter, articulation is a game like the kaleidoscope, and can be varied to infinity. Every syllable, according to the way it is placed, brings its colour. Consonants have different planes of sonority, like the instruments of an orchestra. With a good conductor, one always hears the instrument that one should hear at the moment it should be heard instead of a 'rabble' of sound. It is the same with articulation: the same value must not be given to all syllables, we must know which should stand out and which should remain in the shade. Find, according to the significance of the word, its tonic accent, and put it where it should be. There is something like a pedal within the voice that allows certain words to stand out, to become detached, syllable by syllable, whilst conserving a liaison — for example, 'approfondir', in Duparc's 'La Vie antérieure'.

The mute 'e's must always be open and not closed. If they end a word, pronounce them as little as possible. Refer back to the words to know those that should be pronounced, and those that should not. Pierre de Bréville makes this point very clearly in the preface to Volume I of his songs. It is up to the singer to reconcile the demands of the notes with those of the vowels, for they are often in conflict, as in Fauré's 'Les Berceaux' — 'Les grands vaisseaux . . . sentent leur masse retenue'. The 'a' of 'masse' is placed on an E flat, and is almost impossible to pronounce correctly at the same time as the sonorous amplitude of the note. Whether to pronounce 'masse' exactly by sacrificing the sound, or to make a beautiful sound in sacrificing the vowel — this is the dilemma.

It could be said that, in singing, for every tessitura, each note has a perfect laryngeal position, which is facilitated by a vowel that suits it, or made difficult by a different vowel that does not. Every time the latter occurs, a kind of accommodation that saves both the sound and the vowel must be found. This is the reason for the deplorable 'cocktail' vowel that is at the base of many very good singers' articulation. I think the placement of a voice would be much easier if, first of all, the position where the vowels that correspond best with the student's natural tessitura, and normal emission, were discerned; and then, from there, the positions of the vowels that are difficult for him could be attained. In emission, as in expression, it is always best to take as the basis of our work that which is the most natural to us, and the easiest.

Articulation and expression must supplement vocal

insufficiency. The more the sound diminishes, the more the articulation must become firm and precise. Whatever modifications it undergoes in the course of a work, the articulation must never die; even in the very rare moments where the sound is more important than the word, we must always articulate. To a voice that is naturally sonorous, articulation brings form and variety; and it succours a less sonorous voice by increasing its carrying power. When the sonorous possibilities of a voice cannot respond to the demands of the composition being interpreted, the singer must, more than ever, make use of articulation, and find through it the 'accent' and biting quality that the voice is not sufficient to give.

A beautiful, ample voice always has great difficulty in using the lips to articulate. But why? We cannot do without this first labial position, that is of labial articulation. It must be practised without singing. Wagner, writing to Liszt, urges singers to take the printed libretti and to read their rôles distinctly and with expression. First learn to articulate well in speaking. Many singers articulate badly in singing because they articulate badly in speaking, and articulation is the more important because, for certain singers, it is so difficult to achieve. When I hear students who articulate badly, I ask them to have the kindness to say the first two or three phrases of their piece to me, while I go to the end of the hall. And I find that not one of those whom I reproach with a lack of articulation in singing is capable of articulating clearly in speaking. If we cannot speak with a clear articulation, how can we sing with one? Since everyone is obliged to make use of words, we should, above all, make them understandable, articulate them, pronounce them; for, once the vocalization is added, badly articulated words make it impossible to understand anything at all.

The speaking voice often contains and reveals the faults of the singing voice; thus the emission of the speaking voice has great importance for the singing voice. The habit of wrongly placing the speaking voice is deplorable for vocal emission. In France, especially among men (professors, lawyers, etc.), the low notes of the voice are too often wrongly used.

To 'timbrer' the speaking voice, search first for a kind of 'nasale sonore'. [Editor's Note: 'Nasale' in French has a very different meaning from 'nasal' in English.] If one has not got it naturally, to neglect this placement is to deprive oneself of the most brilliant part of the resonance. Lilli Lehmann, in her *Method*, says in speaking of 'nasalization' that one can never utilize it enough. One of Sacha Guitry's records, studied with attention, will explain better than any words what a 'voix timbrée' signifies. To place the speaking voice, to search for the resonance as high as possible, is the true remedy for fatigue and for an emission that does not carry. If not, no season at a spa, no medical treatment will be any use. Personally, it was on a doctor friend's advice that I searched for my speaking resonance, that which allows me to speak longest with the least fatigue. I tried to raise my voice and I ended by finding my lowest note with the highest sonority.

This true vocal placement must be the singer's ideal. At the beginning of studies, the awakening of the voice must be made on its true place of support, without which we lead our interior shape into absolutely fatal positions. The speaking voice, the setting into motion of all our organs, shows the action by which we shall attain all the notes of our vocal ladder. From the moment we want to sing, from the moment we must speak, it must be done in such a way that there is no fatigue required from him who utters, nor from him who listens. This should be thought about in the colleges and schools. It is a habit that should be given to children — but a child is never asked to tell a story, he is made to write it, that is the mistake.

Racine, in his preface to *Esther*, speaking of the young ladies at the house of St Cyr, tells us that they were made to speak about the stories that had been read to them, or on the important truths they had been taught. They were made to recite by heart, and to declaim the most beautiful passages of the best poets, and that this served above all 'to cure them of much bad pronunciation'. Nowadays, more than ever, with mechanical means of transmission, a well-placed voice and a clear articulation are indispensable. I am sure that articulation is the same in speaking as in singing. In speaking we articulate, in singing we must not cease to articulate. The aeroplane engine turns in the same way when the aeroplane is rolling along the runway and when it flies.

Although our articulation in singing must be the same as in natural speech, in singing, as in speaking, one can say there is a 'Sunday articulation' and an articulation for 'every day'. The tragic actor articulates on a wider and less ordinary rhythm than the comic actor. The articulation of tragedy suits opera; the articulation of comedy suits operetta and folk-songs. Between these two extremes is placed a scale of articulation that varies according to the character of the work, of the text and of the situations. They can be tender, energetic, impera-tive or imploring. Songs call for one or the other, according to whether their character is more or less dramatic, or more or less intimate. An imperfect articulation may not harm (alas) an operatic career. But it is impossible in a career of operetta where the value of the words is paramount. One will never be able to laugh at something one has not understood!

The great classics demand a noble articulation for their true interpretation. For *Werther*, for *Manon*, a correct articulation is sufficient, but for *Armide*, for *Dido*, for *Orphée*, for *Pénélope*, there must be an added degree of nobility. The difference is the same as that between the tones of comedy and tragedy. Many people believe that vocal work is enough to establish this difference. That is an error: it is the style of pronunciation that matters. At the lyric theatres, (the Opéra and the Opéra-Comique) articulation has an importance of the first degree in recitative, sung or spoken. It is by an energetic articulation on the rhythm of the music that the recitative obtains its value. The life of the recitative depends on the speed of the word, on the length and expression of the rests — silences. Recitative is particularly important in many modern works, from the *Martyre de St Sébastien* to Honegger's great contemporary Oratorios; and it is rare to hear it sufficiently well articulated. However, it can happen that excessive articulation may cut the sonorous liaison between words. It must neither chop the word nor cut the sound.

We must not confuse articulation and pronunciation. Articulation has nothing to do with pronunciation. When we articulate well in one language, it is possible to articulate well in another, but it is rare to achieve a good pronunciation in a foreign language. Good pronunciation is more rare than good articulation. Certain paper-boys articulate distinctly and pronounce incorrectly. Pronunciation is the art of giving to all the sounds their exact value. The French vowel 'i' [ee], is rich in vibrations, but we always shut it up, we put a cork in it instead of opening and 'rounding' it — think of relaxation. . . . (For example: Fugère, who does at 85 what he did at 25. He is like a model of sound, completely supple.)

The day that a singer, who has a good 'key-board', pronounces nobly words that are beautiful, he will be sure of his career. Let us love the words that we pronounce, and have a sense of joy in pronunciation.

FOUR

THE POEM AND COMPOSER

I HAVE CHOSEN as the theme for this series [of classes] 'The
Poem and Musician' because it is with the poem that the
composer has to do, and not with the poet, whom generally he
does not know. The composer is the first interpreter of the
poem, and according to the way he has understood it, our
task, as singers, is made easy or difficult. Through the
composer we have the rhythm of the phrase, its pitch, its
intensity, the nuances, the articulation. How much easier than
a line of Racine for which there is no guide, for which Racine
has left not the slightest indication, with which an interpreter
has only to make a mistake to establish a distorted tradition.
Composers who have set poems have done so in very different
ways: some are more-or-less helpful, others more-or-less
misleading. For me, Debussy is the composer who matched
most faithfully the rhythm of his music to the poem. For
Debussy, as for Caplet and a whole family of musicians, the
poem was a series of words set to music according to the sense
that they found within them — [Mme Croiza gave a rhythmic
reading of the first of the *Chansons de Bilitis*, beating time
imperceptibly, in a low voice hardly accentuated, only with
the rhythmic values of Debussy]. I do not know if you feel the
beauty of that last phrase, it quite transports me — 'Ma mère
ne croira jamais que je suis restée si longtemps à chercher ma
ceinture perdue'. As I often say at my classes, when I think
how Debussy spent weeks hesitating over the value that he
would give to a rest, as Baudelaire did over a comma, I find
that singers nearly always deform the values of notes. The
whole of *Pelléas* could be cited as prosody, as declamation. In

the 'Lettre de Geneviève' it is wonderful how the musical rhythm follows the rhythm of the words. What a pity that poets do not indicate the rhythm of their poems by a kind of alphabet of signs analogous to those in music!

Fauré is a true musician — everything that is beautiful awakens his musicality: he is like the painter who, to put himself into the mood before painting, goes to seek his dynamism in the forest. [Mme Croiza reads 'Clair de lune' using Debussy's rhythm.] I only give a simple reading of it, but one could give a real spoken interpretation of it by observing Debussy's rhythmic notation. That is something one could not do with Fauré's. Fauré is inspired by this poem of Verlaine's. A minuet sings within him. He writes it down and the masterpiece is made. But is it possible to read the poem rhythmically, on the rhythm of this minuet? I do not think so. In Fauré more than in any other composer the singer must study the poem apart from the music, because Fauré's rhythm, which is not necessarily that of the poem, would lead him astray. Often, too, Fauré does not respect the 'silences' that the poem would demand. In *Pénélope* one very often misses pauses, rests [silences]. Fauré draws you on with beauty, with harmony, with music, but he sometimes leads you rather far from the poem.

The work that we must do for the poem, we must also do for the music. Strip the music from the poem and strip the poem from the music. Sing the pure musical phrase as a vocalise, exactly as a violinist or a viola player would do, solely to search for the pure musical phrasing before we put words and music together. When these Master Classes have had poems for their point of departure, I find that I pay still more attention to articulation. The greater the poet that a composer has chosen, the more perfect must be our 'play' with the vowels.

We can never be particular enough about the colouring and sonorizing that well-pronounced vowels represent. We may disregard an 'a' where the note must give everything (as in the cry of the Valkyries for instance), but in a song or a recitative we must play with the infinitesimal nuance, this thing that cannot be explained, that cannot normally be heard except by the ear of the French. This quality of the vowel that, in our singing, must be caressed with love. How I should like vowels to be pronounced with love! The greater the quality of the poet, the more we must endeavour to keep the royal nobility with which the vowel must be pronounced; the more we must sing the poem to music placed within the natural range of our voice, where a good pronunciation is possible.

Nothing increases the interest of those who listen to us like the interest we put into the words we pronounce.

In a song there is the poet and the composer. Once everything is in order from the vocal and musical point of view, the tempo, nuances and rhythm, we must think only of the poet. If we think more about the music than of the poetry, we worry about the voice, and about all the obsessive physical difficulties. We must always think of the poet — it is he who delivers us.

The composer creates the atmosphere, we must express it without shutting ourselves up within it.

I shall never repeat often enough that the text must be practised in rhythm before singing it. If it is said simply, intelligently, it reveals the truth of the work. The music stirs us so much, it masks and covers over the meaning, and so, once we are dominated by it we no longer find the truth. By putting ourselves for half an hour in front of a text, apart from the music, we understand what we would never have understood in singing it indefinitely. Music is an impediment to understanding. It makes us more sensitive than intelligent.

We must know our text and our music well enough to be sure beforehand what we are going to do at a performance, and listen to what surrounds us.

If a singer, the evening before he is due to sing, would spend an hour in his room, alone with his poems, everyone on hearing him would say: 'What progress; with whom has he been studying?' And one could reply, simply: 'It is not that he has been studying with someone, it is that he has understood.'

To declaim the poems is the best and the simplest way to find an interpretation that is alive and true — we are singing with intelligence.

The singer hardly ever goes as far as the thought, the sonorous instrument absorbs him so completely. I am sure that if I asked some students whether the poems they are going to sing are sad, gay or tragic, they would not be able to tell me. They only know that the music goes up to G or to A. . . .

I often ask my students to do what I would like all singers to do, and that is to copy for me beforehand the text of what they are going to sing. Those who had never thought about the poet were forced, in this way, to think about him, and discover in the text what they would never have found merely by singing it.

Valéry said: 'What a fine work it would be for a writer to devote himself to one sole subject that he would treat for several weeks and several months in a thousand different ways.' As an interpreter, I say, how wonderful it would be for one poem to be practised with a thousand different expressions, and a thousand different articulations! There should be work on *solfège*, on rhythm, on articulation, on the words, using the intelligence.

The best way of fighting against nerves is to cling to the words. If the thought is on the poem, the face lives, it is the poem that takes us out of ourselves.

In our repertoire we have some beautiful poems that we can serve wholly. There are others that are more mediocre, and in these we must simply seize the passing word without trying to give the great curve of thought. In a very beautiful poem, in some Baudelaire, for instance, there is a curve. The words take their importance only in relation to the whole ensemble. In the text of a song we must distinguish between the words that express the action, and those that escape from the action and, in consequence, are not coloured by it. It is by these words, that escape from the action, that we can introduce variety into the interpretation. As to the words that express the action, we find among them, in nearly all songs, those that indicate the general colour of the work, and that give the 'key' to the interpretation. But the poem must be looked at in order to find them.

When a French poem is set to music by a Frenchman, there should be an accord between the syllable and the note. This is lost in translation — that is why we must always go back to the original text to find the position of musical accents as they have been placed in the original. The translation may put six syllables where there was only one. We may be obliged to breathe three times, and to cut the musical phrase three times. 'To breathe more often, so much the better!' says the singer with a malicious air, but the phrase is no longer respected.

When one looks at the French translation of a song like Schubert's 'Gretchen am Spinnrade', one sees what an incredible number of rests and notes have been taken out or added in, on account of the translation, and it is frightening. So beware of translations. Always go back to the original text. Translation makes the study of detail impossible. A translation never conforms exactly to the written notes. It entails adding, or suppressing, or turning a crotchet into two quavers.

The singer has the good fortune of serving two creators at once — no other interpreter has this privilege. But the ransom is that he will have to submit the technique of his voice to the exigencies of the phonetics of a language that is not his own. This phonetic will create a barrier, and not only for him. A great instrumentalist will travel across the world understood by everyone solely through the miracle of music. The singer will find himself unable to transmit completely, by the sensibility of his art, all that stirs within him, all that speaks within him, if he has to sing in a language foreign to his audience. I myself have renounced a large part of the repertoire: Schubert, Schumann, Hugo Wolf and Strauss, because I have not liked the translations. I have been wrong, no doubt. It is better to take liberties with translations than to sacrifice the music.

FIVE

IMAGINATION AND INTERPRETATION ON THE CONCERT PLATFORM

INTERPRETATION IS THE forgetfulness of self. Imagination can only enrich interpretation if it is backed by an intimate assimilation of the text.

In a concert, the singer is alone with his or her accompanist and the work to be interpreted. He has not the help of any answering character, of any acting, even of any gesture — for immobility is his law. He must simply find in himself his own means of expression within the framework of musical exactitude, musical sensibility, *fantaisie*, beauty of tone, colour of sound, pronunciation and articulation, and facial expression. The artist must use these multiple means of expression with intelligence, selflessness, taste, imagination and vitality.

He must conquer all his difficulties without ever appearing to encounter them — Rameau spoke of 'taking pains not to appear to take any'.

For the concert artist, the work starts from the first note of the accompaniment and does not end until the last note. Above all, never cease to listen to what is being played, including the music that is *not* sung. Never imagine that when you have finished, everything is finished — there is the music that continues, and you must radiate its character right to the very last notes with your expressive immobility preventing the audience from becoming restless before the end. Live during the rests, let them be part of the construction of the work. Once again, sustaining the facial expression until the end of the accompaniment is an absolute rule for the singer. Only 'put out your light' once it is all over and everyone has gone.

I can never say often enough that the public must be kept interested right from the beginning of a work. Very few singers know how to begin with authority, or know in advance exactly what they want to do. An indecisive singer, distressed by his own performance, is terrible. Know how to begin; know how to end; know how to come on to the platform — and how to leave it. Know how to communicate the shape of the work; not to introduce a conclusion where there is none; know the end well in order to establish the beginning.

Know from the start of a song how to interest your audience, how to enter immediately into the subject, to enable your listeners to enter, too. For this, everything must be in place, vocally prepared as far as possible, to enable you to think of what you are saying and doing.

Come on to the platform as though in conversation with someone. Listen to them, imagine them, in order to create the atmosphere of the work. Imagine clearly the scene of the action and the rôle of the character in this action. Utilize the pictures given by the poet, see them, represent them to yourself, evoke them by thinking of them. When you have the good fortune to have Nature as the setting, express her with all her breadth and scope. Differentiate the characters who are invisible from those who are present in this frame of Nature, the night, the whole mystery that surrounds us. Do not shut in open-air songs or restrict Nature's frame.

Not only must the characters be created and given life, but there must be a careful distinction between those incarnate in an aria or in a whole programme. Do not forget to 'change their costumes'.

In an opera, the costume, wig and make-up help the actor to place his rôle. In a concert, besides his voice, the singer has only his facial expression, therefore he must always bring a rôle on to the platform, and always know what it is. Create the person, fashion a living being. For that, a little acting must be introduced into the preparatory work. Do not be afraid, for example, in practising 'Ma poupée chérie' (Séverac), to rock something in your arms, with a loving look. All such gestures or acting must play no part in the performance itself, but it is good to use them in working at it; they help to create the atmosphere and encourage mobility of the face. They must be eliminated afterwards, for a song must not be illustrated by gestures as in the theatre. Remember once again, in songs only make use of the face (apart from the voice, of course).

An experience of acting improves interpretation in an 'active' sense. This is why, in my opinion, it is good to begin by doing some work in the theatre. If one has once been on the stage, and is familiar with, perhaps, getting up from a bench to fly into the arms of a tenor, something of this movement remains, even in the concert hall. There will be less danger of singing lifelessly.

Failing an engagement to sing in opera, I recommend singers always to work at dramatic arias with gestures and then eliminate them for the concert platform. An actress, on the other hand, I should advise to work without gestures, and later only to introduce those that are absolutely necessary.

An essential quality for any interpreter is imagination. He must be relaxed, he must think of the work he is going to interpret, of the person he is going to bring alive, and find, in his own imagination, the scene he is going to describe and that, through him, the intermediary, the public is going to receive. Let your characters live, do not kill them.

An expressive face is always a beautiful face. Perfect interpretation demands, from the singer, an accord between his facial expression and his singing, and this accord must be complete. Facial expression and voice are two pathways that reach out simultaneously towards the same end, and they must be guided in the same direction and confirm one another.

The interpreter's face must be a sort of screen reflecting everything he sings, everything he says. To show others one must first see oneself. If we have the necessary inner intensity, it will radiate, but when our physical appearance expresses nothing, it is because we are not thinking of the words we say. That physical expression follows thought is a law from which we cannot escape. When we say of a singer, 'She has a cold voice', what we mean is, 'She has no facial expression'. A human voice is never cold, but an inert countenance kills life and expression. To make your face live is a habit to be acquired, but once you have the habit of not repressing everything, but radiating it outwards, it is never lost again.

When I hear a student singer, I try to imagine that I am deaf and wanting to learn, merely by looking at his face, what his singing is expressing. For that, the subject must be alive within him. There are two things that worry me when I listen to certain students: if I shut my eyes I do not understand the words, if I open them I see a face that does not express the words.

There are two masks: the mask of tragedy and the mask of comedy. Each one of us by our natural conformation resembles more nearly one or the other. We should be aware of this and make use of it. On approaching a work, before going a step further, we should have already started our interpretation. If we thought of the mask it required and said to ourselves, 'I put on my tragic mask' or 'I put on my comic mask', we could then exploit all the riches of the *intermediary scale*. Let all the life that we can bring to our interpretation be in our faces. But we must not imitate the performer who, having made a mistake and failed to begin in time, said to the composer Bréville, who was accompanying him, 'Forgive me, master, I was constructing my facial expression'. What is needed is not to construct a facial expression, but to make the face *live*. An interpreter's face must be moved first of all by joy — it can darken afterwards, if necessary, but unless the text contradicts it, let it before all else radiate joy! When there is a moment's possibility of having a happy expression, it must be seized. Sadness must only intervene where the interpretation demands it, never as a basis, never as a point of departure.

Respect the alternations of dark and light. In the saddest song, if it is possible, seize the chance of a gleam of joy, of a happy memory, of a relief. I am against sadness in interpretation. Even in a melancholy mood, there can be room for a smile. In art, I detest all that is maudlin. In singing, always think of expressing someone alive, not someone tired. Do not die in singing; the aim of interpretation is to serve, not to arouse pity.

An inert or anguished face is no help against nervous panic; on the contrary, the more you think of what you are saying, the more animated your face becomes and the more you liberate yourself from this panic. Thus the poet takes us out of ourselves in a song, presenting us with pictures, forcing us to express them, obliging us to transport ourselves to where he leads us.

The rule for the interpreter must be variety, light and shade, not monotony. Whatever it may be, in all the arts, there must be variety and imagination: we must not be content with a beautiful voice, we must put into it variety of expression and variety of facial expression. Caplet used to say with three different expressive intonations: 'At a concert, when one hears a beautiful voice, at the first item one says to oneself, "it is a *beautiful* voice!" (admiringly). At the second piece one says to oneself, "it *is* a beautiful voice" (effectively). At the third, "it is a beautiful voice" (in the tone of "it is *only* a beautiful voice").'

Anyone who has not the necessary vocal talents can replace them by intensity of expression. There is even an expressive immobility that is the equivalent of a long pause. For example, the wonderful expressive immobility of the Japanese actors who were recently in Paris.

Facial expression must not be the same at the beginning and the end of a song. It must anticipate the word: do not let it arrive too late. Do not jump on to it, like trying to jump on to a passing horse and catching it by the tail — be in the saddle before starting.

Expression has nothing to do with dynamics. To find the truth in expression make a sketch, improve on it, build it up out of contrasts and with oppositions. No one can interpret in the same mood all the time or without *fantaisie*.

Singers never have enough imagination, never see clearly enough what they have to communicate, and that is the same in a song recital as in the theatre. How is it possible to express Debussy's 'Fantoches' if one does not *see* this scene from Italian comedy? The same is true of his 'Recueillement': it is not enough to sing the words in time; to express it one must imagine the scene, really live it. Too often singers do not bother about this inward enrichment, they are too preoccupied with their voices and thus remain shut up in their profession.

Painters copied the old masters, and composers have done the same. To copy is not to diminish oneself, it is to learn the secret of the masters and to liberate and shape our own imagination. In order to 'clothe' a stage character, we must again seek for knowledge. Let us use our palette of sound as the painter uses his palette of colours.

The instrumentalist is the soul, the brain, the intelligence. It is he who will use the instrument, his voice. We must open our minds, listen, understand, develop ourselves, 'refine ourselves in some way' before being able to interpret in the exact sense.

In art there are things that can be learned, and things that cannot be learned, but much can be acquired by personal *research*. Talent is not enough, it must always be enriched by our inner richness, and for that we must get out of the daily routine. A pupil of even the greatest teacher will never achieve anything unless he adds something of himself to what he receives.

Delacroix wrote: 'In front of Nature herself, it is our imagination that makes the picture; we do not see either the blades of grass in a landscape, or the blemishes of the skin in a pretty face. . . . What characterizes the great poet, the great painter and every great artist, is in fact not only the invention of a striking type, or of a thought; it is his realization, his strenuous personification. It is this power of imagination that concentrates all the characters in one conception, and makes it really exist and take its place as a complete creation.'

It is clear that the imagination is at the base of all the arts, and that one would gain by an interchange between them, an interchange of richness, an interchange everywhere.

In our own domain I would say that singers seldom think enough about imagination. They never see the stage or song character clearly enough — queen or peasant-girl — they never clothe her sufficiently. In fact, we never develop our own personalities enough, never take them often enough out of our poor human cupboard. I think we interpreters look very little within ourselves. We all have a second self within us, the self that responds to beauty, beauty for the eye, for the ear, and in the heart, the soul. We do not light up our little interior light. Delacroix again: 'Why do past pleasures seem in our imagination much more vivid than they were in actual fact? Why do our thoughts linger with such pleasure on places that we shall never see again, and where our soul felt such a state of happiness? Why even (oh sad and cruel part of our nature), does the memory of friends, whom we lament, embellish them when we have lost them? It is because there passes through the mind, when it remembers the emotions of the heart, the creative faculty that takes possession of it to animate the real world, and draws out pictures of imagination. It composes, it idealizes and chooses. We cannot think of them without idealizing.'

I think all this is relevant to facial expression, which depends on inward emotion, inward conviction and true sensibility. If the interpreter thinks of what he is singing, if he is sufficiently convinced of what he says to create pictures within himself, people or landscapes, to look at them, colour them and animate them, his face will become expressive.

I end with another quotation from Delacroix: 'Man wants to enjoy everything, and does not know how to enjoy what is within himself.'

SIX

THE CHOICE OF REPERTOIRE

THE FIRST THING in the choice of a repertoire is to know oneself and — supreme wisdom — to know of what one is capable and what one lacks. We all have capabilities and incapacities.

First of all, in operatic repertoire, it is difficult for us to make a personal choice. We have a voice which classes us as mezzo, soprano etc., even if the classification is not always correct. But the voice is not enough to indicate its use: physical, vocal and intellectual qualities must all be taken into account. In comedy the physique of the actress makes her a specialist in a certain type of rôle: Reichemberg, at the age of 60, still played ingénues; at the age of seventeen I could not have played them!

To women who are making a career in opera and who are very young, I say: 'Be on your guard. Do not allow yourselves to be made to "force" by the repertoire imposed on you.' Age is important, for, even with all the gifts, a singer must resist the temptation of rôles that are too big, taken on too soon.

Unhappily a singer's instrument, the most beautiful of all and also the most fragile, is often entrusted to people who have never themselves sung, who do not know what singing is, such as directors of opera houses or juries at competitions — we are seldom judged by singers. We must, therefore, know how to defend ourselves and not accept a strain that, coming too soon, destroys us. There is also a temptation to imitate the artists we admire, whether or not our potentialities are the same as theirs. The symphony concert repertoire, for instance, demands, before all else, a very powerful voice that can compete with an orchestra. But there are 'half-light' [demi-jour] works that demand sensibility rather than great vocal strength. So begin (if possible) with the 18th century symphonic repertoire, less cruel than romantic or modern works where the demands of the text and the necessary articulation may extinguish sonority. I recommend the young not to sing only what they like, but to sing what is good for them . . . like tablets for the digestion!

We all have natural gifts; let us employ them and know we can always fall back on them and find them in ourselves. The interpreter must strive to acquire what he lacks, after achieving the maximum of his natural capabilities, and should only exceed them as an exception. The tessitura of mezzo or tenor is the same everywhere, but the weight and strength of a mezzo, in one rôle, is not necessarily the same as in another rôle. Mezzo for mezzo, the rôles do not demand the same strength. But if a strong dramatic temperament is without corresponding vocal resources, articulation and intelligence will provide the balance.

When we come to the chamber music repertory, which is very dear to me, I deplore the fact that certain great songs such as Debussy's *Proses lyriques* and 'Le Balcon', and many of Fauré's great songs, are hardly ever sung. Those whose talent is firstly charm, sensibility and intelligence could well confine themselves within a repertoire of moderate sonority; but that those who have great tonal capacities confine themselves to this same repertoire — no! Singers take very little trouble to go in search of their repertoire; they choose what they liked, perhaps, one evening when listening in an armchair. But how much better to know oneself, to use oneself, and to acquire the talent that is above all a balance between enthusiasm and the means at our disposal. That does not mean that one should choose a repertoire too exclusively severe, and want to sing works only of the first rank. We can always, by enthusiasm and talent, give life to attractive lesser works that are nevertheless good music, without necessarily being great works of art, or 'profound'. Think of the repertoire of a Duse or of a Réjane, who made many secondary rôles into rôles of the front rank by their way of playing them. German singers are fortunate to have Mozart, Schubert, Schumann and Wagner, composers with whom they can go round the world. But one must beware of singing only 'to please'. It is important to remain on the plane of works one respects, but at the same time to know how to vary a repertoire. I should like to see the repertoire of singers growing and renewing itself by a more reasoned and enlightened choice, so that music will be better served, and in particular the great works of our French composers that are so rarely heard.

SEVEN

THE PUBLIC AND THE PSYCHOLOGY OF THE INTERPRETER

1. The Public

By its manner of listening, by its response or by its rejection, the audience becomes one of the factors of the interpretation. It could be called the 'human acoustic' of the hall, giving encouragement or discouragement to the interpreter. But the true acoustic is half of our dynamism. A 'dead' hall where the carpets and hangings absorb the sound, kills us — we are sad, and nothing rings. A sonorous hall, that lives, gives back everything. It is the same in life where we give much to some people who receive little, or give little to others who 'respond'.

Let us always come before the audience with a calm physique, or at least with the appearance of tranquillity, outwardly calm even if we cannot master our inward tremors. From the moment the singer is on stage, he must make himself appear relaxed and never look anxious or unhappy. The being who sings must be independent of his suffering, unsatisfied side and always look confident even if he is not. He must appear as a strong person who knows what he wants to do. All progress made while practising diminishes before the public, so he must accustom himself to sing before an audience — one of the principal advantages of the professional over the amateur. The professional must not 'play timid' with the public; but always play with decision, both as a remedy for 'nerves', and also to enhance interpretation; and, above all, he must look the audience frankly in the eye. He must never underline in public a fault that perhaps no one would perceive.

But the public has to be educated, as well, and helped to relax in order to be ready to receive in the same way as the artist must be ready to give.

I attended two performances of *Tristan*: one at Bayreuth two years ago, the other at the Opéra [in Paris] three days ago. The performance at the Opéra was as beautiful as the one at Bayreuth: it was musically perfect, I wept all the tears in my body and came out enriched for ever. However, everyone said it had been more beautiful at Bayreuth. Why do people always say that? Well, it is because at Bayreuth the audience enters into a religious atmosphere of silence and devout attention. In Paris people arrive late, and sometimes talk during the performance. Even at the cinema talkers are furiously silenced, but during music, it seems, everything is permitted.

People who listen to music do not always put themselves into the right frame of mind for what they are going to hear. We well know, we interpreters, that there is a frame of mind for the work we are going to express. But in Paris the audience has not time to put itself into the right frame of mind to receive it. It goes to the theatre in haste, it is restless and is not in the right mood to enter at once into the atmosphere. It comes, in time, under the influence of the music but not immediately. A section of the public may also be blasé — have seen too much — or it may admire only one artist and condemn all others. Then there is the 'snob' public who will only put itself out for fashionable events instead of choosing, through love of music, the artists it can admire and in whom it can have faith: so that many good and great interpreters remain undiscovered.

The public cannot know how much it gives to an interpreter by its attention, by a kind look, by a smile, by the expression on a face; it cannot know how it supports him and 'recharges' him. The interpreter should not pick out an individual in the audience, even though a personality can help him greatly. But he must never allow himself to be 'put off' by a surly face — one of those faces that make a 'short circuit', that discharge electricity — the artist should tell himself that such a spectator may have his own reasons for being grumpy, his own worries, or his shoe may be hurting him. The interpreter must not let himself be constrained by an unpleasant or inattentive face; his enthusiasm must never be held back or weakened.

To sing before the public or to sing without a public is not the same thing. I will take only one example from my memories of Brussels. When I sang *Orphée* at the Monnaie, I was given a copy of an ancient lyre, very beautiful, but a terrible weight. The first time I saw it I said to my director: 'My poor Kufferath, I shall never be able to carry that!' At the rehearsals I could not handle this lyre. At the third recitative I laid it down saying, 'I can do no more, I will take it up again presently'. Yet, at the performance I did not feel it at all. I did not even notice its weight. That lyre is a symbol of all that the public brings to the artist by its presence.

It can happen that the interpreter finds a warmth and understanding in the public, an enthusiasm that allows him to surpass himself, but these moments are rare, and the true artist forbids himself to provoke them. Concessions to the public, or the search for immediate success, are the death of art, and the death of the interpreter. Art that only dreams of applause, abdicates; it places its crown on the forehead of the crowd. I have never thought of the public when I am about to sing. I have never thought of anything but the 'work' and of my possibilities, but not of the public. I try to follow the words of St Francis de Sales: 'Keep yourself always, as far as is possible for you, on the side of simplicity and modesty, the greatest ornament of beauty.'

2. The Psychology of the Interpreter

We have to convince ourselves that to interpret means 'to serve' — and, for us, to serve two chosen beings, composer and poet. So often the interpreter is engrossed with himself, with his throat, with his voice. Speak to a singer who is about to sing, and he will never tell you that he is in good voice — he is always starting a cold or just finishing one, or he has something tickling in his throat. A singer who remains pre-occupied with himself cannot achieve anything. He must forget himself and think only of 'serving', not even of 'collaborating'.

Even so, happy are those to whom a creator will be able to say that in them he has collaborators (as Debussy could have said to the original singers in *Pelléas*). When this is the composer's reaction, it can only be because his interpreters have been faithful to him and have honestly served him, as he himself served the poet. 'To serve' is indeed woman's most beautiful rôle, and those who fail to understand this deprive themselves of the truest happiness. It is the same in interpretation. The interpreter who has made himself study all that the musician has noted in detail, is faithful to his mission. He can tell himself that he has an easy task since he has nothing to invent, nothing to add, he has only to do what is written, and not 'disarrange' anything, to use a word that I like. If, before we go on stage, we concentrate on the words 'to serve' we should soon be relaxed and do our best. Afterwards, let come what may: at the time of performance the only thing to do is to know what we want and to put ourselves into the state to serve well.

I have already mentioned that we should avoid disturbing the public by personal nervousness. The calmer we are, the better our interpretation will be projected. Gordon Craig said, 'Art must be lifted above personal feelings and nervous sensibility'. I wish the interpreter could be like a luminous white screen, ready to receive and reproduce all that the creative artist gives; if the screen adds colours, the task is not fulfilled.

We should gain a great deal if we could listen to others without acrimony, without pettiness. I am always struck to see how a singer at the opera, for example, never hears anything but the rôle or aria that he has performed, that he has sung himself. We should listen with a generous, relaxed heart, and not always judge others in relation to ourselves, to this miserable mirror that we take about everywhere. If we try to know why people do what they do, why they do not satisfy us, then we can enrich ourselves, and our interpretation gains thereby.

Interpretation is like life. We must be able to communicate all aspects, all feelings. If we do not disturb the music, everything must pass through us. We believe too often that success depends solely on what we do, whereas it is the creator who is primarily responsible for success. I immensely admire some German interpreters. But why is it, generally speaking, that German singers have so much success in spite of their unequal worth? It is because of their repertoire: it is Schubert, Schumann, Wagner, it is Bach that we go to hear. Even if the singer has not an incomparable talent, he travels with exceptionally precious luggage! It must also be said that a composer who is still unknown has a poor share of public interest, and it is a wonderful task for an interpreter to be able to gain recognition for such a man.

No interpreter must base what he does on success. He must try to serve his best and in that service, find his joy and his contentment. Nor must he be embittered if success does not crown his accomplished effort. Remember Romain Rolland: 'Let them not complain too much, those who are unfortunate, the best of humanity are with them.' Talent is not enough to climb all the steps of the ladder, there must be many other elements. The public is indignant that a Mme Curie returns unobserved on the same boat as a triumphant Maurice Chevalier. But it must be said that Maurice Chevalier certainly looked after his publicity, while Mme Curie was content with her inner richness — the true wealth of the artist.

I find the following in a book by the painter Odilon Redon: 'What distinguishes the artist from the dilettante, is only the suffering that he, the artist, feels. The dilettante looks only for pleasure in art.' And again, 'What did he do to cultivate his spirit when there were no books? He looked at the universe and at the earth. And in his reading of his work, man formed the most moving chapter.'

We are handicapped, we singers, by our blessed instrument, that derives from the whole of our nature as human beings, that depends on a cold, a chill, on everything. . . . A violin is carefully looked after, preserved from dampness and changes of temperature. We singers, even if feeling unwell, travel, carry our suit-cases, spend nights in the train before singing and must always go on. We never feel ourselves absolutely in good trim. To come on to the stage completely relaxed is especially difficult for us. In the end, however, we have to say to ourselves, 'So much the worse, I will make use of my instrument as it is'. Let us once and for all make a resolution to rid ourselves of our preoccupation with the instrument, to try to attain this generous expression of ourselves by forgetting our terrible self-criticism.

I remember, when I was in Brussels at the beginning of my career, a German company, conducted by Mottl, came to give some Wagner performances. I always attended rehearsals alone in the theatre, and I had the impression that Mottl's gift of himself was so total, so generous, that everything would have continued by the force of his impulsion, even if he had put down his baton. He did not know me, he had no idea who I was, but nevertheless he could not stop himself from turning round and saying to this human presence, 'Beautiful, isn't it?'

The 'Trac' [panic occasioned by nerves] is a kind of vertigo caused by too much importance being given to oneself. To think only of the work is the best way to escape from it. Not to think of oneself, nor of the public, but to think of the composer, of the poet, of what they wished; to think of the mission to be accomplished, which is to serve and not to betray the creators. To forget oneself, to be true. I have often dreamed of a kind of singers' club where we could meet to talk about art and our faults, without hate, without meanness, with love — to learn to receive, to learn to give.

3. Interpretation is the forgetfulness of self
Interpretation in singing is like all the arts, a question of sensibility, of intelligence and of taste, more than of vocal gifts. Interpretation is the mirror of life. The interpreter must express everything, the feelings and the being. But in order to express, he must know, he must love and he must come out of himself. The interpreter is a being who must give much. To

give much, he must have much; to have much, he must know how to acquire. The interpreter must also ceaselessly enrich himself, and this gift of receiving is perhaps the most rare in the interpreter. In order to receive we must try and silence in ourselves the kind of narrow mentality that consists, when we hear someone else, in seizing the side most open to criticism: 'This woman's pronunciation is bad', or, 'she articulates badly'. Do not let us see only the fault, for this woman perhaps has a very beautiful musical feeling, and if we concentrate only on the fault, after half-an-hour it will irritate us. On the other hand, after having stated and accepted the fact that her articulation is defective, if we appreciate her pretty voice, the notes well given, the lovely musicality, we enrich ourselves. Therefore, receive with kindness.

May our art lift us above meanness, above our human meanness, may it bring us a ray of sunlight on a cold day. Let us recognize the talent of others. Let us try to have this magnificent richness within us. If we have not got it, let us try to give it birth, to cultivate it, for it will bring us joy. Therefore, the psychology of the interpreter is to enrich our inner being.

If we do not serve works we do not appreciate at once, we commit, in my opinion, a capital error in not trying our best. An interpreter may not like a certain musical style, but he must serve it nevertheless, for he can be mistaken, and the composer has only one means of bringing it before the public, through the interpreter. If no interpreter can be found, because the composer's taste, enlightened or not, does not comprise certain musical values, the work can never find a judge, critic or public. To interpret well we must love what we do, give ourselves to the work we undertake with all the enthusiasm that is in us; and we have much enthusiasm, often more than we realize. Since I have been giving classes, I am sad to see how many people, inwardly rich, do not dare give out anything of themselves . . . Modesty? Lack of confidence? Education? They end by diminishing themselves and by hiding the best that is within them. In order to exteriorize, there must be a will-power; it is a question of surmounting individual disposition to learn to use the will.

Although the interpreter leaves fewer traces than other artists, his task is a magnificent one, for me the most beautiful of all: to serve and not to consider oneself any more. I wish that all those who sing, who are the servants of the art may feel all that is so admirable in this word. To serve music, to serve poetry. Once our word has carried the poet's word, once our voice has sung the music of the composer, we have only to disappear, our work is accomplished.

4. The Creation of 'Character'

When a singer is on the platform, I always want her facial expression to show me the character that she is to represent. I have just heard the same singer as both Marguerite and Venus. She was neither one nor the other. The same was true in Fauré's 'Chanson du pêcheur' and 'Nell' — they were the same character. The first was not sufficiently sunk in sadness, the second not sufficiently radiant.

The creation of character depends on our own interior. If the character lives in us, it will be there to guide us, to enable us to discover the right intonations, it will be beside us like a kind of mysterious 'double'. But for that, the character must have lived in us beforehand. Once on the platform, it is too late; the character must have taken life from the words which we give it, much more than from the notes. It is by the words, by concentrating on and repeating the words, that the whole life of an interpretation comes.

The character who accompanies me on to the stage is a fictitious one who must completely absorb my own personality. When I am going to sing, Mme Croiza does not exist; it is the character leading me by the hand who must absorb everything. And do not imagine that the most dramatic character is the one that is the most intense: it is not the face actually weeping, but the face that has wept so much that it cannot weep any more, that moves the audience most.

Continuous feminine sadness reminds me of something in

the London music hall. The scene is the parapet of a bridge over a river. A man, passing by, finds a woman weeping and consoles her as best he can, but he cannot get rid of her. At last he succeeds and she goes away. A little later, again passing the same place, he finds another woman weeping, so he looks around to see that no one is watching and pushes her into the river. That is drama! Let us not be the second woman, we interpreters, let us not be this eternally melancholy character that no one can endure, however kind his heart. It is against the tearful aspect that I warn women.

Among one hundred theatrical artistes there are, perhaps, not twenty capable of living their stage characters. To find them, one must go to the music hall. Marie Dubas and Yvette Guilbert know how to live them, and when Yvette Guilbert tells us that she is going to sing a song in which she is sixteen years old, she sings, and she is sixteen.

So let us learn to silence our own personal character in order to listen to the imaginary character who is going to lead us by the hand.

Claire Croiza's Classes

PART II
Songs and Rôles

EIGHT

SONGS OF FRENCH COMPOSERS

1. GOUNOD, BIZET AND CHABRIER

CHARLES GOUNOD (1818–1919)

Gounod left around two hundred songs, with some master-pieces among them. He may well be called 'the father of nineteenth-century French *mélodies*'. There is such a love of the poet in Gounod, such true sensibility, naïvety and ardour, that it is a joy for me to sing his songs.

We will take 'Venise' (the poem is by Alfred de Musset) that shows his care for a charming poem, and his beautiful vocal line. . . . Nothing stirs, the moon and stars are half-veiled in cloud. . . . but now in the moonlight, la Vanina waits, singing in her floating cradle. Narcissa puts on her black mask for the fête — 'Let us leave the ancient clock in the Doge's palace to count the dragging hours. Indolent Venice on the calm sea does not count her days, or her loves. A chain seems like a necklace adorning her beauty.' [After singing 'Venise', Croiza added:] 'I think one cannot deny that the genius of the French race is found in this song and in such sensibility. Gounod is an admirable composer, who is not sufficiently well known today. He is the root of French vocal music. ['Au Rossignol' (poem by Lamartine) followed. Croiza said:] For me, the encounter between Lamartine and Gounod is the meeting of twin hearts; two artists made to understand each other speaking the same language, so pure and so ardent. To come back to colour, I would say that this is the domain of white, the white of purity that can play with the most intense ardour. The encounter produced something paradisial,

77

although Lamartine had written that he always thought music and poetry harmed themselves by associating together. But Baudelaire expressed the opposite view. In 1857 he wrote: 'As a musician has written "L'Invitation à la valse", I wish that a composer of genius would undertake to write "L'Invitation au voyage" to offer to the beloved'. He was rewarded: at least six composers have set these verses to music.

A proof of the importance Gounod gave to the words he set to music is that in 'L'Absent', this next song, he wrote them himself! [There followed 'Dites, la jeune belle', 'Envoi de fleurs', 'Heureux, sera le jour', 'Prière', 'Au Printemps', and an aria from his opera *Mireille* and several other arias.]

I have always wanted to sing a song by Fauré after one of Gounod, so that one can see clearly this same love for the poet that unites them in my mind.

GEORGES BIZET (1838–1875)

Fauré used to say of Bizet: 'Light, sensibility and charm . . .'; and Saint-Saëns of the same composer: 'We differ in everything, following a different ideal, he searching above all for life and passion, and I running after the chimera of purity of style and perfection of form . . .'

It seems to me, Bizet has also the perfection of form. Today one searches a great deal and finds little, and I feel that in earlier times one searched less and found more. I will sing through Bizet's 'Les Adieux de l'hôtesse arabe'. It is a difficult song because it is very vocal and very romantic. It is an entire epoch: I am sure we find ourselves in front of a masterpiece. I will read 'Berceuse' because I have never sung it, but it is a song that I find charming. [See Croiza's talk on *Carmen*, page 151.]

EMMANUEL CHABRIER (1841–1894)

With Chabrier we enter into something quite different. First of all, the two other composers are Parisians, this one is an Auvergnat — less aristocratic, but he brings the healthy roughness of the mountaineer. In Chabrier there is a male quality that a woman singer can never give entirely. It must be a man who drinks well and eats well. There is a basic roundness, and frankness.

I give 'L'Ile heureuse' so that it can be heard, but I am not at all the right interpreter for it. In Chabrier there is a *rubato* which is not in the French character. There is a kind of supple right hand, whilst the left hand 'va son train' [goes on its way], unlike the exactness of a Ravel or a Debussy.

Chabrier is very difficult for the French to sing, especially for Frenchwomen, and still more so for Frenchwomen accustomed to modern music. The qualities needed for Chabrier are the same as those for Brahms, who is never well given in France. There is a loosening in the tempo which is not notated and this necessary *rubato* must be added.

Fugère knew how to sing Chabrier. He brought to it his own roundness, his joviality. But I warn others to be on their guard. In French music, we must make a special place for Chabrier, a special case musically. It is not a phonetic problem, it is a musical one, and not of its epoch. For the liberty allowed to the interpreter is not a modern characteristic.

2. GABRIEL FAURÉ (1845–1924)

I am not going to talk about Fauré and his music in general, many others having done so. I only want to speak of his songs as an interpreter; these songs that are tender, yet virile, never sentimental. They shine with a light that is spiritual as well as physical; they are perfectly balanced and aristocratic in the best French sense, discreet and serene, but full of underlying passion.

And they have a characteristic forward-movement, an 'allant' that has nothing to do with the expression or the nuance. The expression and the colour must be found and interpreted within the 'frame' of the tempo — his *diminuendi* must not be slowed down unless he has so indicated. He has often marked *diminuendi* but, except in his very early songs, very seldom *rallentandi*. Very often we find at the end or climax of his songs, a rise of expression within a *diminuendo*, and so the intensity of feeling must rise within it, and can be helped by the articulation.

Fauré loved the poems he set to music and they formed a musical pattern in his brain which took control of the words. He knew it is nearly impossible to articulate clearly on the notes above the stave, and so he set most of his songs for the tessitura of the mezzo voice.

Let us think of the texts as he did himself, with intelligence and understanding of the words, and with a 'true' articulation.

I beg singers to work at the vocal line as a vocalise, and then spend a fortnight repeating the words away from the music, before singing them with the piano, sensing the harmonies, and fitting text and music together like a glove. They would be surprised at the end of the fortnight to find how much they had gained.

I knew Fauré well and sang his songs with him, so I know what he liked and what he did not like. He gave exact indications in his songs, and yet, in spite of this, the ends of his *mélodies* are nearly always slowed by singers, and in so doing his music is most often deformed.

Fauré himself wrote: 'I want to suggest the great mysteries in the clearest language. To imagine consists in trying to formulate all that one would desire that is best, all that outruns [dépasse] reality — "volupté" has no merit if it does not make us perceive, through the mirage of physical things, an unutterable reality that is beyond the reach of our senses', and Fauré never betrayed that dream.

As you know, there are five song cycles and three volumes of *Mélodies*. In Volume I many of the songs still show the influence of Gounod, with a few exceptions that lead us on to Volume II, where his own voice predominates, as in his lovely 'Clair de lune' [Verlaine] for example; and in Volume III, beside many other beautiful songs, his inspired settings of

Verlaine in Opus 58, often called *Mélodies de Venise*, were written in 1891 whilst on a unique holiday.

In the cycle consisting of the nine poems taken from Verlaine's *La Bonne chanson* we hear his most exquisite uniting of poetry to music. He wished to evoke the thought of the poet, not paint it. He disliked virtuosity for virtuosity's sake, or *rubato* for effect. He would say, 'To move a listener a little, one must be moved oneself ten times more', and, 'Inspiration is a kind of interior song, or mysterious listening—nevertheless, it is right to make an effort, to conquer the laziness natural to man — to try and make clear the thought that wanders.'

Among the poets he chose were Hugo, Gautier, Leconte de Lisle, Sully Prudhomme, Samain, Armand Silvestre, the great Baudelaire and Verlaine, then finally Van Lerberghe and Jean de la Ville de Mirmont.

We must try and enter into the atmosphere he has created, and not allow our own personalities to disturb it. We can never search enough, or try enough to find the necessary purity of vowels. A thorough preparation will enable us to give ourselves up entirely to the impulse and beauty of the music. And when we sing one of his finest works like the *Chanson d'Eve* or the *Bonne chanson* cycles, our appearance, our way of standing and looking is most important. We must make the public feel, and see, that we are 'full' of the work, really inside it, transfigured, reflecting its spirit in our inmost souls. Toscanini was an example of such thorough preparation and rehearsal, every little detail having been worked out with his orchestra beforehand, so that they were able to give themselves up entirely to the soaring impulse, the love, and beauty of the music, and the imperceptible 'balancing' of the tempi.

In his songs, Fauré argued that the voice should not have the 'voluptuous' prestige of a solo instrument, but be a 'porte-verbe' [mouthpiece], with an exquisite timbre. He adored nature and life, but his music is not descriptive, he seeks to evoke the effusions of the night, the secret communion of man and invisible things. He searched for serenity in 'ravissement' [ecstasy].

Vol. I Après un rêve (poem: Romain Bussine)

Fauré's songs are always begun too slowly. I once heard 'Après un rêve' sung by a singer who 'literally died'. The same evening, dining with Fauré, I said to him, 'Finally [enfin] Maître, what tempo do you want for "Après un rêve"?' and he replied, 'Without rallentandos [sans ralentir]!' Fauré did not like the sentimentality that makes his music sound what the French call 'mièvre' [arch or coy].

In 'Après un rêve', 'Tu m'appelais, et je quittais la terre' is a departure. This whole first section is in the same enchanted feeling of a happy memory. In 'Pour m'enfuir avec toi', sound the consonant in 'toi'. 'Lumière' — make it luminous by the diction and by your facial expression. As Valéry says, 'In order to relate a dream one must be wide awake'. Therefore, this song must not be begun as though one were asleep. 'Un ciel éclairé par l'aurore' — women singers always make it 'a sky obscured by storm clouds'!

The tempo Fauré wished was not slow. The awakening to reality comes at 'Hélas!', where there must be a quick 'interior pirouette' with the realization of loss and sorrow, but there must not be any *rallentando* at the end. Give very little tone on the first 'reviens', illumine by colour the 'radieuse', and give nothing on the second 'reviens' and sing 'ô nuit mystérieuse' in the same tempo and *pianissimo*.

Vol. I Chanson du pêcheur — Lamento (poem: Théophile Gautier)
An early song.

'Ma belle amie est morte.' Do not let the beginning suggest an indifferent 'belle amie' just before such a tragic lament. Find the way in your singing to let the voice expand — a certain 'release of everything' that beautiful voices should be the only ones to allow themselves, whereas, in general, one only finds it in tired voices.

So, in this song the beginning should be static, so that you can make the essential big *crescendo* of expression that follows. In recounting his anguish, the poet's sorrow 's'augmente'. We only have a certain range of expression, therefore begin with this 'solitary' sad story that goes away over the sea. Then 'sur moi, la nuit immense plane comme un linceul', torn with sorrow, and declaimed to the immensity of sea and sky, the fisherman recalls the beauty of his lost love and the endless sorrow that reaches the farthest distances of the ocean.

We must be careful not to put 'accents' where the composer has not put any. In reaction against a period in which everything was permitted to interpreters, the new generation of composers indicate everything that should be done — nuances, tempo, expression. We cannot get away from what is written. The interpreter is there to serve the musician.

Vol. I Au bord de l'eau (poem: Sully Prudhomme)
I should like to be encouraging, because whatever we do, with whatever faults we have, we can always do better if we think of what we are saying. This is a young and happy song. It is one of the first of the earlier songs that showed Fauré's own, original, musical instinct. We interpreters have many beautiful poems that we can wholly serve. There are others that are more mediocre, which is the case here, where we must simply sing and seize the word as it passes, without trying to suggest the large curve of a thought . . . and the voice must flow and shape the musical phrases.

After 'le voir fumer' there must be a breath, to mark the new idea and image in the poem. Fauré himself observed the printed musical 'join' that should not be there, and remarked to me, 'I wonder where this bad habit of not "breaking" there comes from?' He had forgotten he had written it without noting the need for a new phrase.

In life, we do not always wear the mask of truth; in singing we must wear the mask we want and whenever possible choose the mask of a happy interpreter. Always look happy to sing, even when that is not so. In life smiles are happy things that light up a face, why do we lose them as soon as we sing?

Vol. I Lydia (poem: Leconte de Lisle)
Another early song, but a complete contrast to the romantic

'Chanson du pêcheur'. Here the Hellenic style of the poem is perfectly captured by Fauré in the lovely, classic curves and lines of his music, that must be interpreted simply and tenderly. The 'mourir toujours', of course, really means 'vivre, aimer toujours', so let your face express this happiness and listen to the phrase.

When we find difficulty in expressing feeling, we can, in practising, change a word in the text like this, to help us find the true expression, and then, keeping the expression, put back the actual word in the text. Work at the poem away from the music.

Do not close the mute 'e's too much, and, at the end of a word, lighten them.

Vol. I Ici-bas (poem: Sully Prudhomme)
Make the contrast in each verse, the contrast between what is, and what the poet dreams of. The rhythm should have a slightly rocking motion. 'Je rêve' — *piano*, but happy!

Vol. I Dans les ruines d'une abbaye (poem: Victor Hugo)
Do not miss a certain spice of malice here. 'On s'en va . . . puis encore'. Underline the conclusion, 'C'est l'histoire des oiseaux, dans les arbres'. It is not difficult to take breaths in singing; the skill lies in the expiration of the breath; to have enough and give out little.

When a character comes on the operatic stage, we know if it is a gay or a sad character. I should like to get the same impression, away from the theatre, from singers on the concert platform.

Vol. II Nell (poem: Leconte de Lisle)
This must be clear, gay and happy and make full use of 'charme'.

'Ne fleurisse plus ton image' — first time, full of 'entrain' [enthusiasm], second time, *pp*, but without allowing the expression to diminish. Very supple and phrased exactly as Fauré has written it.

Gabriel Fauré

Vol. II En prière (poem: Stéphan Bordèse)
Simplicity — faith.

A child's prayer, some say the Christ-child's prayer. In any case, it must be sung as a prayer in solitude not as a performance.

Vol. II Les Présents (poem: Villiers de l'Isle Adam)
I am beginning to think we do not hum enough in singing, we do not sing with enough relaxation. 'Je t'apporterai des colombes . . .' These doves should be a charming gift, precious, soft, pure. . . . This must be suggested by the lengthening of the words. Do not cut them off short.

Vol. II Les Roses d'Ispahan (poem: Leconte de Lisle)
This song must be sung without any effort. The gently rocking movement must be very relaxed, oriental, very languorous and very much 'in love', imperceptibly swaying, no rigidity.

Vol. II Les Berceaux (poem: Sully Prudhomme)
Sing this more for its drama than its charm. The picture must be visualized at once: the large ships going very far away, with the small cradles very near. The idea is beautiful and the contrasts must be made. It is not a charming distinction that is needed, but a tragic opposition between the two. And in this modern French music there must be a pitiless tempo with a rhythm that never changes, but is supple. There must be variety, which is achieved by a verbal enunciation with an articulation that communicates the intensity of the expression without changing the intensity of the sonority or spoiling the shape of the musical phrase. Do not neglect the commas.

This must, however, be kept as a *mélodie*, not sung as an operatic aria; but its intimate character must have reality. Let it begin in a port, see it, evoke it. Then imagine the men who must search the far horizons, and the women who must stay with the cradles — the adventure — and the anguish, 'sentent leur masse retenue'.

Express the 'déchirement', the anguish. The 'a' of 'masse' is difficult. Make it short and hard, not long or deep.

Vol. II Clair de lune (poem: Paul Verlaine)
To begin, is to enter into the scene with someone who speaks to you. You must listen to the piano before the voice enters, and put yourself into the appropriate atmosphere. Fauré should be worked at with a metronome; he wants absolute fidelity to the tempo indicated. Work at the words *in tempo*, without singing them, and at the musical phrases as vocalises, then sing the two together.

'Et leur chanson se mêle au clair de lune.' Make this moonlight poetic, but not operatic. Respect the note values without exaggerating them. Never look unhappy when you sing this. Always look at ease, even if you are not, and never appear to have finished a song where the voice part stops, it only ends with the last note of the music. Remain in the atmosphere. Let your bearing prevent the public moving before the end.

Here moonlight intensifies the poetry. It releases something. It is a shaft of light that appears, and changes the colour of the *mélodie*. We are no longer with the other Watteau figures, but detached. . . . This detachment is perhaps even more underlined by Fauré's music than by Debussy's. 'Marbres' — pronounce this word well to the end with all its value.

Fauré is a musician. All beauty stirs his musicality. He is the artist, who, to put himself in the right mood before painting, goes for a walk in the forest. But it is his own dynamism he goes to seek, not that of the forest.

Vol. II Le Secret (poem: Armand Silvestre)
I always hear this song sung by women, and it is always made too sad. There is a curve towards daylight that is never suggested, everything remains in a tepid, feminine twilight, whilst there is the dawn, the morning, the day, a whole progression. . . . 'Que le jour proclame . . .', then the sunset.

The curve is in the poem; it is there, too, in the music, but it is above all by the rests that the curve is communicated.

'Aux plis de sa robe pâlie . . .' — impossible to take a breath in this phrase.

I never tire of repeating that there is a lack of variety in art as there is in life, and as there is in the theatre. And I know that it is impossible to live always in the same monotonous, unvarying colour. The singer hardly ever goes all the way towards the poet's thought, he or she is so absorbed by the sonorous instrument. I am sure that if I asked some singers whether the poems they are about to sing are sad, gay or tragic, they would not be able to tell me. They only know that the melody goes up to a 'G' or an 'A'. Since in life we do not remain at the alphabet stage of writing, but go on to style, why should we remain at the stammering stage in singing?

The contrasts in this song are so clearly marked, we have only to follow the poet and the composer. Singers are docile, but lazy. They allow themselves to be led, and never seek for themselves. The great singer is the one who has found the best way to make use of his own, personal instrument.

I have always dreamed of listing the various points in singing on which everyone is in agreement. There are very few.

Vol. II Automne (poem: Armand Silvestre)
[To a male singer]: The title of the poem is an indication of this song, not 'furious' but calm and broad, with a feeling of melancholy. (Do not leave out commas.) May all rejoice whom I have reproached for the habit of melancholy!

Here, as I said, we interpret a feeling of melancholy, which does not always mean 'sadness'. There is a melancholy that comes from a happy memory. In this memory there is a whole musical *crescendo* that is nearly always neglected. It is really a colour of feeling, like 'Il pleure dans mon coeur', that does not exclude charm, even if it is darker. Let your face 'live', do not kill, or repress this inner 'second self'.

If Fauré had orchestrated the rise of the music at its climax, there would surely have been a chord of triumphant brass. We must find this sonorous chord in our interpretation and communicate it.

Be careful of the 'e' *muets*, do not close them.

Vol. II Poème d'un jour (poems: Charles Grandmougin)
  (i) Rencontre
[To a Polish student]: Too sad! 'I was sad, I met you, I am not sad any longer —'. This is a declaration of love.

[Student]: There are French fine points I do not understand.

[Croiza]: A declaration of love is the same in all countries. The words may be different, but the feeling is the same, the tone is the same. This must be illuminated, radiant.

  (ii) Toujours
The interpretation should not be angry! It is a declaration, fiery and rising, rising, rising. But it is a question of articulation, not of sonority. Follow the impulse given by the piano, listen to it, answer it, 'jump on to the horse' *in tempo!*

  (iii) Adieu
This should not be sung too sadly. Never render a song more tragic than it is. I see this song with a spice of humour, of irony. Finish it rather as 'See you again, and thank you!'

As we are all women here, I will tell you something. We must beware of our feminine nature which always gives a little more than is asked for. In love, always, in friendship, often . . . 'monde léger . . .', do not multiply the 'l'. This makes it heavy; *pp* . . . Adieu . . . final *pianissimo*. A *pianissimo* note must be expressive, not a meaningless *pianissimo* made for its own sake, with arbitrary pause of the voice.

Vol. III Opus 58 — Often called 'Les Mélodies de Venise' (poems: Paul Verlaine)
Because Fauré would not compose to please the popular taste, he was never prosperous in a material sense, and composed during the summer vacations. But, knowing his pride, a group of friends arranged a lottery, designed for him to win,

and that enabled him to spend a holiday in Venice where he conceived this Opus 58, to poems of Verlaine, and these are among some of his most exquisite songs.

Mandoline
The poem and the music closely recall a Watteau painting and an eighteenth-century scene from an Italian 'Commedia dell' Arte'. From the very beginning we have a tempo that will not change, that must not change, although there is a very slight *ritenuto* on the '(ra)*mures chan*(teuses)', then *a tempo* again.

The gaily dressed couples serenade and dance beneath the trees in moonlight of pink and grey. The whole picture must be light and supple.

En sourdine
All these poems of Verlaine and Samain, above all when they are set to music by Fauré or Debussy, have a quality of happiness that must be communicated. There are two masks, the mask of tragedy, the mask of comedy. Each one of us has an instinctive affinity with one or the other. We must be aware of this and come to terms with it.

This song is a nocturne, half asleep and calm, and the two key words that suggest the colour and must be interpreted here, and sung simply, are 'silence profond'. It is a happy, not a melancholy silence.

Green
The text, and therefore the verbal enunciation are most important in this song and I cannot recommend you too strongly not to sing it slowly. The mood is lively, almost breathless, young and full of genuine emotion, not sentimental. Above all, sing this for yourself to someone.

Fauré once said: 'I have no wish to cradle the reveries of others by my music'. In other words, 'volupté' and restraint.

With the freshness of morning dew still on his brow, he brings her fruit, flowers, green branches, and above all, his heart. 'Do not let your white hands tear it,' he says, 'but let my humble present be sweet in your eyes.' So the 'd' of 'doux' is important, and the rest of the lovely youthful love-poem is matched by the tenderness of the music.

À Clymène

An enigmatic poem of mystical 'correspondences' evoked by the poet's beloved, and set to a fascinating musical pattern.

C'est l'extase

In a sense, the end of 'Green' is the beginning of 'C'est l'extase . . .'. There is an almost lethargic tenderness and languor between the two people in this lovely poem, identifying themselves with all the scents and sounds of surrounding Nature. Fauré's markings are explicit and terribly difficult to follow because of this 'forward movement' within which all the nuances, the poetry, the subtlety and the ecstasy must be realized.

★

La Bonne chanson, that Mme Croiza sang so often, several times for Cortot and with the Pro Arte Quartet, was originally set for voice and piano, but Fauré was persuaded to make an arrangement for voice, string quartet and piano, though later he said he preferred the original setting for voice and piano.

From the 21 poems of pure joy, that Verlaine wrote during his engagement to the young Mathilde de Mauté de Fleurville, Fauré chose nine.

The whole of Verlaine's *Bonne chanson* is a poem of love and of radiant happiness to come, a shedding of the past and imagined unclouded joy — these settings are some of Fauré's most beautiful songs, tender, subtle and restrained, but with an undertow of passion, and radiant with happiness.

The descent . . . will come, but as Fauré has not put it into the music, we are not obliged to express it. The sadness of Fauré's interpreters is terrible! and he is sung more often by women than by men.

Gabriel Fauré

La Bonne chanson Opus 61 (poems: Paul Verlaine)
  (i) Une sainte en son auréole
  In this first song, Fauré expresses the poet's tender pride in
his beloved's likeness to the 'noble ladies of ancient times',
immortalized in mediaeval stained-glass windows, and in her
Merovingian name, and her youth and freshness.
  In the repeated F flat, Fauré evoked the 'golden note of the
hunting horn'.
  From the beginning the singer is describing a succession of
enchanting visions; but at 'Je vois, j'entends . . .' a sudden
change of colour and expression must make it clear that this is
the key to all these poetic evocations.
  The dynamics rise only twice to a *forte*. The first and very
quick *crescendo*: 'de grâce et d'amour' has its climax on the
B flat of 'mour', not on the E flat of 'et'. The fast tempo must
be maintained to the very last bar of the song.
  (ii) Puisque l'aube grandit
  In this poem there are three different emotions: of exaltation, hope, and the firm decision to walk straight ahead,
whatever life may bring; of the supreme happiness of walking
this road with his beloved; and of 'single, simple airs'. It is an
ascent towards happiness. It is not even a week after the
marriage, it is before. It is radiant with hope, happy, happy,
happy. 'Puisque, puisque, puisque . . .' up to a paradise that
must be higher than the ceiling! This paradise is devoid of
sonority, but has a great rise of expression. To make it
understood, one could say, 'It is twilight, I only love you the
more. Night is falling, it is not because of this that I will love
you less.' The nuance here, 'S'apaise', softens, but that does
not mean that the inner self or the expression are less intense.
And, I repeat, this song gives a wonderful example of Fauré's
expression that must remain independent of the tempo and the
dynamic nuances.
  The unfortunate Fauré has indicated *senza rall*, so sure did he
feel of a coming catastrophe. The change comes in the piano,
from semi-quavers to triplets. And at 'Et vraiment je ne veux
pas d'autre paradis' we must rise with our whole soul for the

expression within the *diminuendo* and *piano*. The interpreter must be penetrated absolutely by his inner vision of the work.

(iii) La Lune blanche

Maintain the initial tempo all the way through. Keep this beautiful line, this lovely vision that has no hint of sadness. There is no *ritardando* at the end, and yet a singer only has to have a good F sharp for the accompaniment to 'slow-up and die' on 'C'est l'heure exquise', and the performance is ruined. Nevertheless, Fauré was quite aware that an 'heure exquise' cannot last for ever, and he gave it a limited duration!

(iv) J'allais par des chemins perfides

The occasional harshness of the harmonies expresses the memory of a past he means to shed, and his determination to lead a new life.

(v) J'ai presque peur en vérité

[To a student]: 'Do not sing this like a tired old gentleman!' As it progresses, this poem of hope rises to white heat. At the beginning it is relaxed and warm. In 'l'avenir doit-il m'être sombre' do not let the word 'sombre' have too immediate an importance. The curve of the spoken phrase must be controlled. Individual words do not always have an instant value. If we feel obliged to give them one, it is generally because the poem is inferior.

Singers never think enough of the direct look, 'regard'. We must make use of it and not invoke the sky, where there is no response to be found!

I am certainly among the interpreters of Fauré who adopt the fastest *tempi*, and yet the composer himself often found I did not go fast enough. So, when I sing Fauré, I always pencil on my accompanist's copy, 'faster', 'mouvement métronome', because I know that the moment there is a *pianissimo* the conductor or the pianist will slow up. But of course, there must be no question of anything being distorted by being too fast. We must follow the composer's own indications.

(vi) Avant que tu ne t'en ailles

This is perhaps the most difficult song in *La Bonne chanson*, because of the two 'parallel' poems, so beautifully contrasted by Fauré in tempo and feeling in his music, as they are by the poet.

(vii) Donc, ce sera par un clair jour d'été
A poem of happiness, sunshine, love and hope; again, on 'chère beauté', a *diminuendo* with intensity of feeling, and at the end a slower tempo but with an increasingly rapt tenderness of expression. This seems a unique characteristic of Fauré.

(viii) N'est-ce pas?
A lighter mood, almost carefree in the innocent enjoyment of their love, companionship and indifference to the outer world.

(ix) L'Hiver a cessé
In this last song of the cycle, Fauré has to such a degree put the accent on the overflowing joy of the poet's summer, of this awakening of love that it is impossible not to express it.

Vol. III Prison Opus 83 (poem: Paul Verlaine)
This tragic poem was written in prison: the awful monotony of the prison round, the glimpse of sky, of the tree, the sound of the church bell, and of the bird singing its lament through the tiny window. And then the sudden realization of the life outside that he has forfeited, and asking himself: 'What have you done with your youth?'

Again, nothing operatic, but an intense inward tragic understanding.

Vol. III Soir Opus 83 (poem: Albert Samain)
This is a poem of 'bonheur grave'. In life both gaiety and happiness co-exist, but it is possible to be gay and unhappy; so we must insist on this 'deep happiness'.

This wonderful *mélodie* begins with a beautiful musical line. At the outset it must not be too full of light, it is a nocturnal, warm, enveloped atmosphere. At the start of 'Soir', I always have the feeling of opening a window after the rain and walking out on to garden paths, of hardly daring to speak, so 'captured' is one by the atmosphere, an atmosphere that must be communicated by breathing in the freshness of earth and burgeoning flowers.

'Voici que les jardins de la nuit vont fleurir . . .'. Do not change the tempo. The four semi-quavers of the accompaniment should be maintained all the time with the absolute precision of a metronome. There must not be a *crescendo* until after 'C'est la pitié . . . Tes yeux levés au ciel . . .'. This 'ciel' must be like paradise, a round sound that demands a 'pedal-covering' like the 'rendaient pareils, le soir . . .' of Duparc's 'La Vie antérieure'.

'Les jardins de la nuit . . .'. Think of a summer garden in the evening, of the smells, the peace. 'C'est la pitié . . .' is not a pitiful pity. This 'pity' of Samain and of Fauré is a departure for an ascent, and in this rising *crescendo*, Fauré rises with the poet, and this 'montée' must be made something wonderful. It must not be done like a speaker who, in diction, would use too low a voice. It must rise in line with the rhythm, the tempo, these four quavers that must never change.

'Tes yeux, si tristes et si doux', impeccable tempo and articulation of the 'd' of 'doux' that creates all the final atmosphere, the impression you will leave with your audience. The singer's facial expression should radiate joy. It is impossible to give too much importance, too much love, to the way we pronounce this 'si doux', this consonant 'd' that is so important in French. Let us be creatures who enrich, who give happiness, even if it is necessary, for the expression, to darken occasionally. This is a song of 'bonheur grave'.

How rare it is to find a pianist who, like Jean Doyen, plays the four semi-quavers evenly throughout!

[Note: At one of her recitals, Mme Croiza read the whole of Samain's poem 'Elégie' from which Fauré put the last three verses to music under the title 'Soir', and which she sang after reading 'Seul le soir sur les routes', with the accompaniment starting, without any interruption, straight into the *mélodie*.]

Song cycle 'La Chanson d'Eve' Opus 95 (poem: Charles van Lerberghe)
In this beautiful cycle, there is from the beginning, an awakening of Life. '. . . La jeune et divine Eve s'est éveillée de

Dieu . . .' Fauré felt the importance of this so deeply that the
piano is silent, and he really leaves the singer alone to
discover the nobility of expression needed. Breadth and
nobility of articulation are essential here. Everything must
keep us wholly in Paradise and prevent us from falling back
on earth; an immobility that nothing must disturb. We must
keep ourselves in this atmosphere without anything of our
own nature transpiring and disturbing it. It is terribly
difficult, not vocally, but to interpret. Our interpreter's soul
will never seek enough, or search enough to find the purity
of tone it demands. It is through detail by detail, and in
making the curve of the work, that the interpretation must be
constructed.

La Chanson d'Eve is certainly one of Fauré's least well-
known works. I hope that everyone leaves here with the
desire to know it better, then the mission of the interpreter
who has just sung it will be fulfilled.

When we sing a magnificent work like this one, our aspect,
our appearance, has a great importance. The public must be
made to feel and to see us full of the work, radiant through it,
and reflecting in our person, the spirit of the work.

3. HENRI DUPARC (1848–1933)

Duparc was an artist in the whole acceptance of the term, not
only a musician; he also painted and wrote. His correspondence with Chausson, concerning the latter's compositions,
sets forth many of his ideals. Duparc was one of the generation
of composers who wrote exactly what they wished done. He
said to me one day: 'If I had known what some singers do with
them I would never have put any *rallentandi* in my songs'. He
looked for suppleness, softness without loss of timbre, and, in
such songs as 'L'Invitation au voyage' and 'La Vie antérieure',
for the mystery and the longing for a dreamlike beauty evoked
by the poems.

Duparc's *mouvement* is always full of life and the lack of this quality is the fault that I find with most interpreters. A girl once came to sing to me 'L'Invitation au voyage' and I said in a joking way, 'Go on, go on, I shall overtake you!' That is it — singers slow down the tempo and do not respect Duparc's vivid accentuation, tempo and *mouvement*.

I am afraid that I am going to speak about myself. In 1914 I went to see Duparc at Tarbes, with Mlle Meedintiano who was accompanying me on that day. I sang nearly all his songs to him, and I must tell you that his joy came from hearing them sung in time, with life and in the right tempi. Owing to his tragic illness, his sixteen songs are the only lasting compositions that ensure his immortality.

L'Invitation au voyage (poem: Charles Baudelaire)
In an article on 'L'Invitation au voyage' Reynaldo Hahn made a great error of judgement against the refrain, 'Là tout n'est qu'ordre et beauté', and I mention this because people are so often like sheep, and approve without discussion what has been said by someone else. This is not the way to judge.

One day I heard a great French musician, whom I will not name, demolish Wagner 'root and branch'. There was nothing left — I said to him: 'My poor friend, I know an old spinster who has a horror of the sun, a horror of daylight, who lives with closed shutters — but nevertheless the sun exists! Happily!'

I do not know if Duparc ever knew Baudelaire's remark: 'A musician has written "L'Invitation à la valse", but who is going to compose "L'Invitation au voyage" and make of it a song that one may offer to the beloved, to the chosen sister?' If Duparc did not know this remark, and yet fulfilled Baudelaire's wish so completely, the song seems perhaps even more beautiful.

I do not wish to speak for too long, but I do want to quote some words of Mme Duparc. After the death of her husband she sent me a small pastel of his that I had much admired on my visits. It was done in Switzerland on one of the lakes he loved. It shows a very calm corner of the lake, a very calm sky, a

semblance of cloud, an atmosphere . . . a nothing. In send-
ing it to me, Mme Duparc wrote: 'This is one of the last
essays from his hand, and also the last effort, may I say, of his
poor dear eyes from which the light was escaping little by
little, almost like the last rays of the setting sun.' Duparc had
the joy of a companion who followed him, understood him
and served him to the end. When I told her of my admiration
for her, she protested and said, 'But what greater joy can
there be than to serve a man with such a spirit?' I always came
away from the Duparcs deeply moved.

People so often take pleasure in showing up the pettiness,
the meanness of great artists, that I feel that it is good, on the
contrary, to bring out the beauty and the grandeur of one of
them. If many creative artists are not understood, it is often
the fault of their interpreters, the fault of those who do not
know how to see or understand. In French music Duparc is
one of the most virile and healthy composers. This man who
was ill nearly all his life (I do not know if he was already ill
when he wrote these songs), nevertheless is, in his compositions, strength and health incarnate. Let us try to give
him the place of authority, of power, of virility that belongs
to him, and let us not try to be among those who fail to
recognize great music because they are unable to understand
it.

Take first 'L'Invitation au voyage' — if only we made this
as radiant as it should be! But it is often made a melancholy
thing, and the poem is never given enough life. It must be
sung with all the happiness inspired by Baudelaire's vision of
a marvellous journey together — since there is a feeling of
departure about it, it makes a good end to a group.

Neither spinelessness, nor a 'feminine' sentimental approach will do here; you know I detest everything self-
pitying in interpretation. This is a man speaking, someone
who goes right to the end; it is virile — not affected. A few
details: in 'leurs larmes' the 'a' is not easy on that note, or to
keep perfectly in tune. Practise it by brightening it imperceptibly from a deep 'a'. In vocalises, big things are often

practised, while little things are neglected. On the contrary, the small sonorities should be sought.

'Là — tout n'est qu'ordre et beauté!' Do *not* slow this up, the composer himself has marked 'un peu plus vite'.

'Luxe', an 'e' mute that dies away; 'calme' — ca-alme, with 'volupté' in saying the consonant 'c'; 'et volupté' — let it come out, not 'wrapped up' and do not 'die' in singing!! Underline the 'v' in volupté and in saying this you must look radiant with 'volupté', Baudelaire's 'volupté'.

'Bout du monde' — whatever our strength, it is never enough by itself to express the 'bout du monde'. No power could suffice; so suggest it by the softness of the consonant — all very intense effects must be given in this way, by softness and by contrasts that express much more than power, that would never be enough.

The beginning must not be too slow, start with something alive, a live desire, a call. The second verse a little faster, and there must be a nuanced progression up to this joyous flowering of sound at 'Les canaux, la ville entière'.

There are three ways of singing 'L'Invitation au voyage': there is the good way — I am not speaking of that — there is boredom, and then there is the sermon; but it should be an invitation — a voice alluring us away.

The speed always flags. 'Tes traîtres yeux' is the only *poco rit* marked in the whole song. But do *not* slow up on 'Là — tout n'est qu'ordre . . .' this must be sung with happy ardour, with enthusiasm, with happiness, with the certitude of departure. Here, more than in any other song, our own feelings must help us to find the right verbal accent — even when it is not indicated.

Now a minute criticism of Duparc. After 'd'hyacinthe et d'or' the musical phrase continues, while the phrase in the poem is finished, but something else is beginning. There should be a break here. The criticism is infinitesimal, but in some operatic works it is tragic when the music continues while the action should stop with the text. Samain said, 'Poetry could not do without a rhythm, as fluid and as little visible as possible; but through this submerged shape, one must still feel the latent presence, the vague, lost rocking of the music, as when, in a motionless boat, one vaguely senses the gentle drag, the almost imperceptible but irresistible depth of the current, and the entwining sweetness of living water.'

This admirably expresses the need of movement of sound, of the indispensable interaction, the constant inter-relation of energy and suppleness. Our inward enthusiasm, our face, never accompanies enough the poems that we sing. All the more reason for it when enthusiasm must 'draw' someone, as is the case in 'L'Invitation'.

Modesty is splendid, but terribly chilling for what we express. Every time that we do not conquer modesty, everything shuts itself up again in our interpretation, as one sees flowers shut themselves up at the slightest contact in a natural history film.

Phidylé (poem: Leconte de Lisle)
Before you start singing, I have to tell you that, in my view, 'Phidylé' cannot be sung well by a woman — the ending is impossible. There is a 'waiting' and a force that we cannot give. I said this to Duparc one day, when he asked me if I sang it, and he replied, 'No one has said that to me before, but it is true. In composing it, I thought of a man.'

Many times I have seen 'Phidylé' announced by female singers I greatly admired. I said to myself, 'Ah! at last I am going to hear it as it seems to me it should be'. But it never was.

The primary wisdom of an interpreter is to know his limits. For practice, we should work at everything, and most of all at what is contrary to our nature — let the gentle and sweet practise tragic songs, the tragic natures sweet ones. But to perform them, to interpret, we must know and respect our limitations. Not only must we be master of our physiognomy and not deform it, but still more must we radiate, bring the radiance of that other being that is within us, the one that vibrates to beautiful things. But sentimentality, that terrible fault of women, leads us to deform the opening of 'Phidylé'. It should be radiant with the intoxication of the heat of a summer's day.

'L'herbe est molle au sommeil' — do not begin to awake, but sing with eyes almost closed. The face should be completely relaxed, happy, natural, saying it almost as if stretching inwardly. 'Repose, ô Phidylé' should be loving and warm. If the face is not in harmony with the words, the 'Repose' becomes an order! The thought must be on the words for the face to be expressive. 'Midi sur les feuillages rayonne': think of this noon warmed by the sun. In this exquisite poem, nature has the first place; the sensation of summer that we have within us, that we kill if we do not give it with imagination and with sufficient thought given to the text.

Then comes the awakening, with its tremendous curve of expression. I cannot understand the fault of melancholy or excess of sentimentality applied to Duparc's music that is so virile, that has vertebrae, that always goes the whole way. The song is written for a man or for a great soprano. I am not a soprano and cannot sing the end as I feel it.

Chanson triste (poem: Jean Lahor)
This is not a sad or lonely song, it is a song for two, and therefore less sad than it seems.

'Je me noirai dans ta clarté . . .' make this 'brightness', this 'light', consoling, living — 'que, peut-être, je guérirai' — a 'perhaps' full of hope. The end is a succession of *pianissimi* full of expression, all expressions of tenderness and love where nothing must 'fall', but be intensified. Search for the expression of this tenderness in your own world, search for your own tenderness. Always take as the base of your work that which is familiar to you, that which is natural and easy for you, in the expression as in the vocalization.

'Parler de nous' — an offering — 'I have been ill, but you are here, you hold me, I am better, I shall be cured'. To interpret, we must exteriorize, we must bare the soul. The first time it is not amusing, but it must be done whatever it costs: the soul's tenderness, faith, enthusiasm — everything! We must give everything, and then our interpretation becomes alive, and we find moving sonorities — simplicity, warmth, love of the work, and rhythm, strength, nuances, colour and movement, these with expression are different things, and not tied together. And the nuances above all must be distinguished from the others because they colour everything.

Au pays où se fait la guerre (poem: Théophile Gautier)
This song of Duparc's is dramatic. The three verses must be varied and different from one another. In the recurrent 'Et moi toute seule en ma tour' it is the gradation from the first to the third that is difficult. But all the drama is in this gradation.

The first verse is a statement of facts. There is not yet any dramatic intensity to give — 'To the land where the war is being fought'. 'En partant', on leaving, a kiss of farewell, sad, but not yet tragic, yet something different from the preceding verse.

The second 'Et moi toute seule en ma tour' — the beginning of anxiety, the hope, despair — 'des pigeons': cooing of the pigeons on the roof. 'I feel near to weeping' — the anxiety is intensified. The footsteps that gave hope, the despair at seeing only the little page.

The third 'Et moi toute seule en ma tour' — 'Vents du soir' . . . hope is at an end. He will never come back, he has been killed.

Let us tell ourselves that the intensity of the sound has nothing to do with the dramatic intensity of the words. And do not bring the drama too soon; do not let everything be finished before it has begun. Let us begin with life and hope; the drama will follow.

[And to another singer:] 'I await his return all the time' — his return, where is it? Has it remained in the copy? What is missing in what I have just heard, is that there is neither beginning nor progression nor end. [Mme Croiza analysed and acted the poem phrase by phrase, and added] It must go from progressive anxiety to final despair. But how can we give it if the scene does not live within us, within our thought? It was da Vinci who said, 'How can one express the contraction of a face if one does not feel it?' One more proof that there is only one rule for all the arts, and that Life is at the base of everything.

Extase (poem: Jean Lahor)
Written by Duparc purposely as a tribute to Wagner's *Tristan*. There must be a straight, tranquil line, a deep lake, on which there is not a ripple.

Le Manoir de Rosemonde (poem: R. de Bonnières)
The articulation of the beginning must be bitingly virile. The end, from 'En passant par où j'ai passé', up to and including, 'le bleu manoir de Rosemonde', should be dreamy and sad.

La Vague et la cloche (poem: François Coppée)
This demands the articulation of a noble bass voice. The waves and the bell should be given with two different rounded and powerful sonorities. The poet describes how, after strong drink, he dreamt he was helplessly drifting in a rudderless boat on a wild sea, without a light or hope of reaching the shore. The dream changes to an old bell-tower and he is astride the huge, cracked bell, swinging to and fro, making the old stones tremble. The singer and the music are dramatic and powerful.

Then he awakes to a melancholy reality, a change of colour and expression in the voice, and asks the dream, with anguish, why it had not told him of the true pain of existence.

Lamento (poem: Théophile Gautier)
The scene is an isolated little cemetery, the singer beside a white tomb among the black cypresses. The beginning suggests semi-obscurity, without life or colour. The tempo must be absolutely even, a monotonous declamation, with only the two short *crescendi* indicated. Begin with a calm and expressionless grief; grief can make you weep, but grief goes much deeper and further than tears. This grief, here, where

suffering has taken everything else, leaves a motionless serenity that has no need of words. This immobility creates a silence that has an immediate effect. Then comes the intense *crescendo* in the piano part and quickening up to 'Ah! never more . . .'. The piano sustains the quicker tempo until the last three bars when it reverts to the slower pulse of the opening.

Sérénade florentine (poem: Jean Lahor)
Very light, lyrical and supple, visually a charming little serenade. The poet invokes the evening star to bless his sleeping beloved, asking the dawn to bring a star of love to her thoughts.

La Vie antérieure (poem: Charles Baudelaire)
The last song Duparc wrote. It opens with a beautiful, imagined memory. The composer gives us an atmosphere that must be expressed without the singer being enclosed in it. For Baudelaire, the beginning of the 'La Vie antérieure', the words 'J'ai longtemps habité', is a wonderful, distant memory of a previous existence, searched for from far away. It is about to unfold itself. We must express the distance and suggest something that rises up little by little in the imagination.

We must be with Duparc and Baudelaire in their domain, enter into their vision, live it with them in order to be able to evoke it. At first we have the marvellous evocation of the beginning, and then follows the painful return to the realization of self ['le douloureux retour sur soi'].

We must create the picture —
'J'ai longtemps habité sous de vastes portiques . . .'
'Les grands piliers droits et majestueux . . .'
'Rendaient pareils le soir . . .' comma after 'pareils' in order for 'le soir' to have its nocturnal colour, its round, open sonority.
'Les houles, en roulant . . .' a different picture.
'Les tout puissants accords de leur riche musique' must be beautiful, and full of warmth in this wonderful, rich *crescendo* with a quickening of tempo to its climax — 'C'est là, c'est

là . . .'. The two should be separated and quite different. The second 'c'est là' repeated in another colour, more secretly, and 'que j'ai vécu' held back and becoming *mezza voce* both in voice and expression. For 'dans les voluptés calmes' suggest a calm delight. 'Volupté': this word is so dear to Baudelaire that one finds in nearly all his poems; it will not do to pronounce the 'v' of 'volupté' like that in 'virginie', and yet 'virginie' can be a beautiful word too.

'Au milieu de l'azur' — all this must be mysterious, and, as indicated, 'in a vision'. 'D'approfondir' — the marvellous chord on 'dir' must be matched in its harmony by the voice as if the singer put a foot on the sustaining pedal: it must be astonished, an expression of wonderment and the pain of the return from such a journey back to the self. To do this we must leave our human anxiety, and just sing Duparc's music exactly as he has written it. And the attack on the 'd' in 'approfondir' should be slightly held back.

'Le secret douloureux' begins a curve down to 'qui me faisait languir'.

Above all the song must be lived. It is not something immediate, of the present moment, or that has happened an hour ago; it is a progressive awakening of memories imagined long ago and far away.

4. ERNEST CHAUSSON (1855–1899)

[Chausson composed about 40 songs as well as larger works, and was most generous to young composers, including Debussy. A fervent disciple of César Franck, he became a great friend of Henri Duparc, to whom he submitted many compositions for criticism. He dedicated *Poème de l'amour et de la mer*, for voice and orchestra, to Duparc, and asked for his opinion on it. Duparc replied, 'It is in fact an exquisite little work, and I am happy to see my name figuring at its head', but went on to say that he was not quite sure about some of the declamation, and did not wholly approve of the soprano

version written above in red ink. He accepted variants of a
note or two, but not a change of melody to the same
accompaniment. 'If a soprano wants to sing what was
intended for another voice, a mezzo, let her transpose it, but
even so! . . .' This distressed Chausson, and Duparc had to
reassure him, saying that he had only remarked on the
declamation for the sake of Chausson's future vocal works. He
felt that declamation in a song should be more as it would be
without music, and not give the impression that the words had
been adapted to the music, or that there was not an absolute
cohesion between the two.]

[Five songs from the volume containing his Opus 2 show a
remarkable understanding of the voice, and great variety of
mood. They are charming melodies, and Croiza always spoke
of the musical phrase, the *bel canto*, the vocalise:] By vocalise I
mean a syllable sung at any pitch to arouse one's musicality.
One should vocalize in listening to oneself. Work at the
nuances. Sing your scales with *diminuendi* and *crescendi* and
with that 'something' between the notes which prevents them
from being mere exercises in *solfège*.

No. 1 Nanny (poem from Leconte de Lisle's 'Poèmes antiques')
Here there is an important curve, a departure and an arrival,
and the singer must husband his emotional power at the
beginning in order to keep something in reserve. Lack of
accent, lack of respect for its 'curve' easily kills the song. There
is a quality of light that can only be attained by starting from
the opaque, by husbanding and slow graduation.

This song is a simple, deeply felt lament. The poet calls on
Nature and the seasons to weep with him for the loss of his
beloved.

No. 3 Les Papillons (poem: Théophile Gautier)
This song is light, lively and full of gaiety. It calls for a clear
bright articulation within each of the musical phrases, up to
the final tender vocal *ad libitum*; and the accompaniment at the
a tempo as light *pp* and *ppp* as the imagined flight of the
butterflies themselves.

No. 7 Le Colibri

Remember that Leconte de Lisle's poem is about a humming-bird, not an elephant! It must not become too sad, it needs imagination and a beautiful quality and supple phrasing, rather than great quantity of voice.

Evoke the colours, the pictures and the warm atmosphere of the poet. There is a *crescendo* up to 'vers la fleur dorée . . .' where you can expand; but make the comma after 'il descend' so as to alight gently on 'se pose'. The warmth continues for 'et boit tant d'amour . . .', in the long *ritardando* and *decrescendo* to 'rose' and the pause. Then *a tempo* and *piano* for 'il meurt . . . tarir' — *ritenuto* for the pianist at the end of the bar. Then *a tempo* to the end, the composer having marked all the nuances.

Apaisement Opus 13

A beautiful calm setting of this lovely poem by Verlaine — less well known than that by Gabriel Fauré.

Serres chaudes Opus 24 (poems: Maurice Maeterlinck)

For a long time I underrated these settings of Maeterlinck's texts; and then, when I had worked at them, I was filled with enthusiasm for, and learned a lot from them. It is a song cycle, that is to say a whole, and Chausson has constructed the order of his songs without losing sight of the fact that they are a suite, with intense colours and intermediary shades. In a 'cycle' do not let us betray the author by modifying his order and suppressing the intermediary shades which he judged indispensable. For example, the 'Serre d'ennui' and 'Oraison' should never be sung one after the other.

The music of the cycle *Serres chaudes* has a quality of enthusiasm [élan] that is not very common in French music; to speak in depth of this work would need a detailed study of the text which might repel some singers, however modern. Certain words are difficult to attach to the music (for example 'les chasseurs d'élans devenus infermiers'). But if a singer cannot find expression in the words of a text, there is no need to cry 'how miraculous!' like the people in Hans Andersen's story of the Emperor's clothes. What does not emerge from the words must be sought in the music, and it is this that Chausson gives us.

Cantique à l'épouse Opus 36 (poem: Albert Jhouney)
In this song, there is deep happiness and if the words are pronounced sadly instead of being expansive [épanouies] both poet and composer are betrayed, and the *crescendo* of the work is destroyed. In reality there is no sadness, here, but a noble happiness, something common in poetry and rare in life.

Chanson perpétuelle Opus 37
I picture the speaker in Charles Cros's poem as a kind of Ophelia, a very young girl, simple and unspoiled, with a personality like Garden's Mélisande. Ophelia then, and not Donna Elvira. Be careful not to make her older, or more mature than she is. It is not a question of physique, but solely a question of interpretation. The beginning must not be sung in a quavering or dramatic manner, so that a listener might think 'In a love affair it cannot have been very amusing!' This is always a danger in recounting the pains of love.

At the beginning there is a whole 'white' section, Ophelia about to die. 'Bois frissonnants, ciel étoilé . . .' She is addressing Nature and there is no human witness of her despair; she is almost numb, asking the winds to tell her lover she is dying.

Then follows her story of a first love that has turned to tragedy. With simplicity she recalls happy memories and, although she is suffering, her face must express her joy in the memory of their love, their meetings, her unguarded avowal, her selfless surrender — 'Et puis, je ne sais plus comment, il est devenu mon amant . . . Je ne dormais bien qu'en ses bras . . .'. Keep it pure, do not be afraid of the words that must be spoken from a virgin soul, a pure soul. Such things only become indecent if we make them so.

Now comes the break between happiness and tragedy, the division, the drama — he has gone — 'Mais lui, sentant son coeur éteint . . . S'en est allé l'autre matin . . . sans moi et dans un pays lointain.' It is one of those things impossible to say, because it is too tragic, but it must be expressed. The commas must be felt. Vary the colour of the voice for the words between the commas, or in parenthesis.

What follows, 'Puisque je n'ai plus mon ami,' must be given with total lyrical generosity, an intense heightening of expression, dramatic, illuminated, each *crescendo* becoming more intense.

All this is dictated by the poet. The song demands great vocal powers and great dramatic ability. Singers who do not possess the 'orchestral' power required, must make up for this lack by intensity of expression and feeling.

5. CLAUDE DEBUSSY (1862–1918)

Debussy is the greatest artist among musicians. To interpret a poem set to music by him is a marvellous experience. He has caught the poet's rhythm so perfectly that the poem can be declaimed without changing anything in the rhythm. The rise of the music and the rise of expression go together; the expression matches the nuances; the intensity of the two is equal.

Ariettes oubliées 1888 (poems: Paul Verlaine)
   (i) C'est l'extase
   This is the first time I have heard 'C'est l'extase' and 'Green' [see below] consecutively, and my immediate reaction is that 'Green' should be ended as 'C'est l'extase' begins. There is a kind of circle that connects the same sensation and the same semi-lethargic character.
   Sing the musical phrasing of 'C'est l'extase' as a vocalise — wide, expansive. Pay attention to the quality of the 'a' in 'C'est la fatigue amoureuse', not 'fahtigue'. We know only too well how much expression depends on pronunciation of the vowels. Both Debussy and Verlaine are equally responsible

for this exquisite evocation of Nature surrounding two lovers who feel their souls are one with it.

(ii) Il pleure dans mon coeur

This song depicts the melancholy of someone inside a room, looking through the window at the rain falling outside. It is a human being, not a singer, wondering why his or her heart feels a kinship, weeping without any reason. 'What? No betrayal? No reason for mourning? To be without love or hate, is perhaps the worst pain of all, not to know why my heart feels such sorrow.'

(iii) L'Ombre des arbres

Verlaine and Debussy headed the song with a quotation from Rostand's *Cyrano de Bergerac*: 'The nightingale sits on a branch of a tall tree thinking she is drowning in her reflection in the water beneath'. In this song, especially, the light and dark of the voice must be on the same plane. The more the sound dies away, the more forward must be the articulation in order to support it. If the articulation provides no counterbalance, everything fades into obscurity, and nothing more is heard. So the articulation must never die.

Debussy has perfectly interpreted the poet's parallel description of the scene and the human traveller; the singer has only to follow and feel the notation as nearly as possible. The *crescendo* and *poco stringendo* are important, then back to *tempo primo* and *piano*.

(iv) Chevaux de bois (Paysages belges)

Above all, the accompaniment must not drag and must be in time. If, in this song, we mentally replace the voice by an instrument, it would be a trumpet. Therefore we must not use too singing a tone, but articulate and try to express the different scenes and people at the fair by vivid imagination. The phrase 'Clignote l'oeil' is an example of the close attention to be given to Debussy's markings, to what is 'lié' [bound, *legato*] and what is not. And 'L'église tinte' suggests a change of mood as well as of tempo; do not attack the high note on 'tinte' too closed — make it more 'tainte' like a bell.

Follow the rhythms, *tempi* and accents faithfully.

(v) Green (Aquarelles)

Several musicians have set 'Green' to music, but for me no other has expressed Verlaine so well as Debussy. 'Voici des fruits, des fleurs . . .' suggests a race through the early morning dew — young, impetuous, stirring — the tempo lively and forward-moving. Do not 'sing' this phrase too much, but on 'Et puis voici mon coeur . . .' bring to it your own intensity of feeling, do not let it be part of the bunch of foliage! 'Souffrez que ma fatigue . . .' a little held back, 'à vos pieds reposée . . .' held back still more, then faster at 'rêve des chers instants . . .' and 'qui la délasseront . . .' slower, with a 'stretching' sensation: Debussy attached great importance to this clearly marked *rubato*. Sing a long 'dé' gently accented, in 'délasseront', and a caressing expression in the *andante*. Your articulation, your diction and the evenness of your notes will enable you to abandon yourself to the love and joy of the final phrase, 'Et que je dorme un peu, puisque vous reposez', eyes closed and reopened, quite naturally.

(vi) Spleen (Aquarelles)

Verlaine took this word from the English, and here Debussy has expressed all this anguish of doubt, despair and rejection of everything but 'You!' Just try to follow his indications and feel an interpretation of the poem within yourself.

Cinq Poèmes de Baudelaire 1887–89

In these *Cinq Poèmes* there is an extraordinary variety, a fluctuation, a moving forward, a holding back, something voluptuous, something bitter, something cruel, all the nuances, all the alternating light and shade wonderfully caught by Debussy. The songs need a voice of ample range, able to give the listener the impression that they are easy, and that the singer is not obliged to exert himself unduly but has a facility that can master the nuances and achieve this difficult tranquillity.

In addition to the purely musical angle — these songs of Debussy are difficult by reason of their tranquillity — there must be enough suppleness to allow for other difficulties, such as the long phrase that must be finished with a smile, or with the ease that is equivalent to a smile; otherwise the interpretation is not right. Both poet and composer demand an ease that necessitates long study. First, the work of learning the words and music with absolute accuracy which, once done, must be put aside to allow the seed to germinate. Then, by forgetting everything, the singer is free to think only of finding the right expression, the complete interpretation.

In these five songs, the complete accord between the singing and the accompaniment must be like the exchange in a stage dialogue. It is no more possible to sing them without this accord, than it would be possible to play a part without being aware of the lines of the other actors.

(i) Le Balcon

This song needs a voice with a very extended and dramatic range, able to express a wide variety of emotion. Debussy's markings must be faithfully followed. He tells the singer and pianist all they need to know.

(ii) Harmonie du soir

Here we enter a domain that is very beautiful but extremely perilous for the interpreter. There is a fluctuation, a ceaseless movement, a life expressed by Baudelaire and followed with genius by Debussy. Here we leave the domain where the word has the foremost place, where it can supply everything. The utmost beauty we can give is not beautiful enough for these two great magicians.

There must be a musical curve, but the poetic curve and the musical curve must first be worked separately. The music must be practised like a magnificent vocalise, like a Kreisler seeking to serve a magnificent musical phrase, in fact, *bel canto*. Vocally, Debussy demands as much as Rossini. It is not possible to reproduce the cohesion of his musical phrases without that *bel canto* that gives to the music, to each phrase, to each note, a true musical value to make them live; for the note is nothing if it is not nourished by an inner life.

In 'Harmonie du soir', at every return of the phrase, 'le ciel est triste et beau comme un grand reposoir' the stanza is broken. But this refrain must again find its musical equilibrium, its inner beauty.

I do not know if the beauty of this song can be taken in at the first hearing. But as we familiarize ourselves with it, we feel its growing beauty, and are able to measure Debussy's wonderful harmony against the poet he serves.

(iii) *Le Jet d'eau*

This is one of those songs that place their characters in a setting. All the time we experience simultaneously the alternation of the two elements — the two characters and their surroundings — love and nature. We must treat differently what is dialogue or addressed to one person, and what is background or 'frame'. Make it clear which of the lovers is speaking, as well as both the time and place.

Here the expression of intense love is always concerned with night, the fountain, and 'la plainte éternelle qui sanglote dans les bassins'. 'Le Jet d'eau' is a poem of love, a dialogue between two people against a background of nature, the night, and mystery that extends far beyond them, and should be sung with an intense expression of love and beauty.

All the way through the rise of the music is on a par with the rise of expression. They are inseparable, although the nuances of sonority, the nuances of feeling, and the *tempi* remain entirely independent and must be distinguished one from the other by the art of interpretation.

[Mme Croiza gave a detailed analysis of this song.]

A poem 'à deux' — Debussy indicates 'languid' — and the beginning, up to bar eleven with the two characters, should be enveloped in an atmosphere of immobility, as if half asleep — 'Tes beaux yeux sont las, pauvre amante . . .'. The musical curve of the phrase is so exactly what it should be, that it helps us to pronounce the words as they should be pronounced.

At bar 12, 'Dans la cour le jet d'eau qui jase . . .', there is a change to an outside element, Nature, the setting for and far beyond the two humans. The greater the difference between the two elements the more authoritative will be the interpretation. In bars 20 and 21 the sonority of the music takes the lead;

let us be carried away by it, be borne along by the sound that creates everything.

Bar 22, *Più mosso*, 'La gerbe d'eau . . .' should be fluid like this jet of water, fluid like the musical design . . . This stanza occurs three times and is given a different rhythm each time, as if the composer had sought to place a different breath. We must follow him exactly in each of the rhythms. Breathe after 'gerbe d'eau'.

There is a *ritenuto* on bar 33, and on bar 34 — 'Ainsi ton âme qu'incendie l'éclair brûlant des voluptés . . .' — a return to the characters with enthusiasm, with life, with ardour, but ardent with tenderness — articulation! If it is true that every poem contains key words, this is the key, and the most intense and characteristic expression of the whole poem. More than ever, musically, there must be precision of rhythm, of tempo, of the nuances. *Crescendo* up to bar 42 where the tempo goes back to *andante tranquillo* and a *diminuendo*.

In bar 47, 'Qui par une invisible pente . . .', an intermediary phrase introduces the following one. The *diminuendo* of 'descend jusqu'au fond de mon coeur' with a *ritardando*, brings the *pianissimo* but *poco mosso* of the second 'La gerbe d'eau . . .'.

Bar 63. *Meno mosso tempo rubato*. Bar 64, 'O toi que la nuit rend si belle . . .', suggests a new transition from Nature to the human element, only to return to Nature before the end of the stanza with bar 70, 'Qui sanglote dans les bassins', and *ritardando* into bar 73, *più lento*. This must be very clearly articulated.

Bar 74, 'Lune, eau sonore . . .', after 'Lune' a comma and a rest, 'nuit bénie', comma and rest before 'arbres qui frissonnez autour. : . .': The way in which 'frissonnez' is pronounced is of great importance. A continued *crescendo* of expression counters a continued *diminuendo* of sonority up to 'Est le miroir de mon amour'. After the preceding intense rise of expression it seems that there is something like a platform of calm.

Bar 83 where 'La gerbe d'eau' (*andante tranquillo*) appears for the third time on a different rhythm from the other two, do not increase the difficulty in distorting the phrases, but remain rigorously faithful to the writing.

(iv) Recueillement

In this song, singing the words in time is not enough to express them. The singer must visualize the scene, he must live it. He must enrich the gift by his own inner richness, and to find that he must leave daily routine. Most singers neither separate the character enough from themselves, nor bring out the character far enough from their poor human cupboards.

'Recueillement' must have this difficult tranquillity above the underlying feeling. The beginning is marked *Lento tranquillo, tempo rubato — molto sostenuto* but *pp* in the piano part 'for the town enveloped in a dark atmosphere that brings peace to some (*diminuendo*), and care to others.'

'While the vile multitude beneath the whip of pleasure,' *poco crescendo* and *animando*, 'This merciless executioner, goes to gather remorse in the slavish fête', *diminuendo molto* and a *ritenuto* back to *tempo primo*, 'My grief, give me your hand — far from them — See! the dead years in outmoded dresses leaning from the balconies of the sky; see, smiling, regret rising from the depths; the dying sun going to sleep beneath the great arch. And, like a long shroud trailing in the East, hear, my dear one, hear the night that approaches.'

'Marche' is on a very difficult G sharp. Try it on an easier vowel; I practised it on 'i' [ee] for a year until it was placed once and for all.

Fêtes galantes I 1892 (poems: Paul Verlaine)

(i) En sourdine.

'Calmes dans le demi-jour.' This is nocturnal, a calm nocturne, half asleep, and it must be sung simply, evoking and joining Nature with the two lovers. I think that in all the poems we sing, we could find two words that suggest the colour that the interpretations should have; here they are 'silence profond'. These words give this colour (compare

Fauré's *La Bonne chanson No. 1* where 'la fierté tendre des nobles dames d'autrefois', a 'tender pride' gives the colour).

Follow Debussy's notation and expression marks exactly, do not lose the tenderness with the quickening tempo of 'ferme tes yeux à demi'; and the whole of that section ends with a slight *crescendo*. In the return to the slower tempo, ending with 'voix de notre désespoir, le rossignol chantera', do not let the F of the nightingale cease to be soft and expressive.

(ii) Fantoches

This is a joke; it is mischievous, witty, full of lightness, irony and different colours. For your characters think of the Commedia dell'Arte, and give them life, otherwise Scaramouche and Pulcinella will be in costumes that are a failure. Plan and vary your 'la-la-la-la's' and watch Debussy's markings of *staccato* and *legato*. The first group after 'gesticulent noirs sous la lune' should be sung in a rather deep voice; the second group, after 'se glis-se demi-nue', lightly and suggestively; and in the third group, the first 'la-la' very lightly with its *piano crescendo/decrescendo* and the last 'la' *piano* with a *decrescendo* to *pp*, but darker in colour, after 'tue-tête'. And be sure to put the accent on 'tê–te' with a vanishing 'te'.

To revert to the characters: after Scaramouche and Pulcinella, the worthy, elderly Bolognese doctor enters, slowly picking pinks; while his lively, pretty little daughter 'se glisse demi-nue' beneath the trellises, looking for her handsome Spanish lover, whose distress is poured out by a lovesick, full-throated nightingale. I think singers, too often the prey to vocal anxiety, create problems in this ending, which in reality is not difficult. The *mezzo-forte* 'clame la détresse à tuetête', *pp subito*, which must be sung as if the singer himself shared in the farce, with humour and rhythm. It is not sentimental. You should declaim this poem in strict rhythm, as though you were acting in an Italian comedy — otherwise it is dull; work on the rhythm of the music. If you lose the rhythm, the backbone, what is left? A song without animation, without gaiety, without life.

(iii) Clair de lune

This needs a tone that is not too supported, but rather 'suspended'. Note Debussy's *legato* phrases, and his notation. At 'tout en chantant sur le mode mineur' do not lose the articulation when the pace quickens for 'Et leur chanson se mêle au clair de lune . . .' but back to *tempo primo* and a change of colour at 'Au calme clair de lune, triste et beau'. For me this moonlight intensifies the poetry; it unleashes something, takes us into a new atmosphere where we are no longer with the other characters, but detached. 'Marbres' must be pronounced to the end of the phrase with its full value and expression that keeps its intensity whilst the sound diminishes.

Proses lyriques 1893 (poems and music by Claude Debussy)

(i) De rêve

The beginning is a dream indeed, very *legato*, soft and expressive, lovely curved phrases. The regret for the beauties passing by, neglected, frail, and old. Even the old trees weep with their golden leaves beneath the golden moon!

Then comes a martial episode with a more marked rhythm. No more golden helmets will be dedicated to them, the helmets are tarnished, the knights are dead on the road to the Grail.

At the return to the first tempo, with its harp-like accompaniment, soft hands seem to stroke the soul, hands so wild and frail (*en animant*) from the days when swords sang for them, strange sighs rise from under the trees. Again a *tempo primo* at 'My soul, you are in the embrace of an ancient dream'.

(ii) De grève

In 'De grève', there is a gust of wind at the beginning, calm and appeasement at the end. 'And the moon comes with compassion for us all. . . . She comes to calm this grey conflict . . . white silk at peace!'

(iii) De fleurs

In these songs the accord between the voice and piano must be established like the 'réplique' [dialogue] in an acting rôle. One can no more work the melody in isolation than act a rôle ignoring the réplique of one's partner. None of us, whoever we are, ever brings enough difference, enough variety into our interpretations.

[To a student]: Here, the 'ennui', the spleen, was good, but the bitterness was not there; nor the nostalgia of the artist that breaks out, the cry of despair that no longer needs the beauty of sound. I cannot find the great curve of anguish in your interpretation. I find the beginning, and the end, but not the centre of what is there. In 'Mon âme meurt de trop . . .', 'meurt' is the culminating point of the sonority and it must exceed the others.

For the anguish, it is indispensable to make use of the articulation. Whatever kind of voice we have, it cannot suffice, for certain very intense feelings, without the help of the articulation. There is a triumphant side, a 'Valkyrie' call in these songs. You have not enough self-confidence to give this. Dare to make more contrasts, and criticize yourselves less.

In our work, we can never be too meticulous in our researches. Caplet searched endlessly with all his fingers, one after the other, for the right sonority of a note. But in singing, in performing, I would say: Let us make mistakes with serenity! 'I am in the water, I am swimming, perhaps I could have made the stroke differently, so much the worse, the race is on, too late to begin again.' The interpreter must know how to make a mistake with authority!

(iv) De soir

Rhythm! rhythm! for the gay, happy beginning to this song, catching the joy of a free Sunday! Even the mechanical joy of the trains running fast; and the impressions of the signals. And then, at evening, my blue dreams sadly recall 'dud' fireworks and the mourning, dead Sundays. The night, on velvet steps, comes to put the beautiful, tired sky to sleep; and it is Sunday in the avenues of stars. The Virgin, gold on silver, lets fall the flowers of sleep. Quick! little angels, outstrip the swallows to get absolution as you go to bed! Take pity on the towns, take pity on the hearts, you, our Lady of gold on silver.

Debussy has marked his words and music so clearly, we must just try and sing what he has written!

Les Chansons de Bilitis 1898 (poems: Pierre Louÿs)
Debussy met Pierre Louÿs in Mallarmé's salon, they became
great friends and had daily discussions on the relationship of
poetry and music. Debussy chose these three poems from
Louÿs' 25 *Chansons de Bilitis* which were supposedly trans-
criptions from an ancient Greek poetess, Bilitis, but in reality
his own — though with a wonderfully authentic atmosphere.

Pierre Louÿs' poems call for music (unlike Mallarmé's) and I
will even say that through Debussy's music his words take on
a different cadence. For Louÿs the Bilitis are sisters of
Aphrodite, for Debussy they become sisters of Mélisande,
through a quality of purity on which Debussy insisted. He
often says to me, 'These *Chansons de Bilitis* are a perfect
example of complete unity between the rhythm, and poetic
and musical declamation, everything perfectly matched. They
can be spoken in the exact rhythm of the music.'

(i) La Flûte de Pan
[To a student]: Your Bilitis is in mauve or black, I see her in
white, pure — not yet having lived, not a full-blown flower,
not 'swooning' but fresh and very young. I speak of Debussy's
music, not 'after' Louÿs. Do not take away the ray of light that
shines on all the Bilitis. The beginning must not be sad. I
divide this song into two. The first part is a kind of recitative,
where the word must occupy the foreground, while the
second part is purely musical for the voice and the instrument.

(ii) La Chevelure
More passionate than the other two. Think of the two
speakers: a little more depth for him; but she is very young,
keep her simplicity. If you follow Debussy's careful dynamic
markings and his rhythms, the nuances will be there. 'Tendre'
must be very tender — but no *rubato*.

(iii) Le Tombeau des naïades
Here you need all the warmth of your voice, of a 'cello
quality' but again without losing the simplicity; no grandiloquence. Again there is a dialogue between Bilitis and her
shepherd. But this time it is she who is looking for him, and
she recounts, 'I was walking through the wood covered with

frost, my hair in front of my mouth glistening with little icicles, and *my sandals were heavy with muddy lumps of snow'*. [Croiza used to say she felt this underlined phrase was the key to Bilitis' feeling of the stress and realization of his distance from her.]

The shepherd teases her belief in satyrs and nymphs, saying the little hoof marks in the snow are those of a goat; but after the phrase that suggests a tiny cascade on to a chord of tenderness, he invites her to rest by the tomb of the Naiads. He breaks off a piece of ice from the stream where they used to laugh, and peers through it at the pale sky.

Fêtes galantes II 1904 (poems: Paul Verlaine)

(i) *Les Ingénus*

Sing the beginning on the semi-quavers, using a clear, crisp, forward-placed diction. The young men, with a subtle mimicry, and light, clear tone, are slightly self-mocking.

At the 'double moins vite', *legato*, they see the autumnal evening light fading and, listening to the murmurs of the young girls hanging on their arm (*lento*) their souls tremble with delighted astonishment.

(ii) *Le Faune*

Very pronounced diction, and rather menacing: the first three bars of the opening accompaniment are *rubato*, then far away but very rhythmical, the sound of distant tambourines. 'The old terra-cotta faun laughs ironically in the centre of the lawn, no doubt foretelling a sinister future to these tranquil moments that have led us, melancholy pilgrims, to this hour whose fleeting seconds turn and turn to the sound of the tambourines.'

(iii) *Colloque sentimental*

[Note: When asked how she would advise a student to sing Debussy and Verlaine's 'Colloque sentimental', Croiza said: 'Everything is in the imagination and facial expression — how can it be explained?' But I saw and heard her sing it several times, and her interpretation evoked this extraordinary creation of two geniuses — Debussy's directions and rhythms matching the poem so perfectly, one felt the icy cold of the listener, straining to see. 'In the old, deserted, frozen park, two forms have just passed by. Their eyes are dead and their lips are flaccid, and one can scarcely hear their words. In the old, deserted, frozen park, two spectres evoked the past.' The dialogue: 'Do you remember our ecstasy of long ago?'

'Why do you wish me to remember?'

'Does your heart still beat faster at the mere sound of my name? Do you still see my soul in dreams?'

'No.'

'Ah! the beautiful days of ineffable happiness when our lips met!'

'It is possible.'

'How blue the sky was, and how great our hope!'

'Hope has fled, defeated, towards the black sky.'

So they walked among the wild oats, and only the night heard their words.

'The mist surrounded the two ghosts as they faded into the distance.'

Mme Croiza gave the opposition between the two voices, she said to her they were 'Hope and Negation'. Playing for Croiza at a concert, Debussy asked her to repeat this song, the only time he had wanted to hear it twice, he said. She never repeated it of her own volition.]

Trois Chansons de France 1904
    (i) Rondel (Charles d'Orléans, 1391–1465)
   (ii) La Grotte (Tristan l'Hermite, 1601–1655)
  (iii) Rondel (Charles d'Orléans)

(i) Rondel: 'Le Temps a laissié son manteau'
This must be full of sunshine, joy and light. No clouds must be put in it! To sing with charm is good, but even charm must not remain too monotonous. The public says to itself at first, 'This singer has charm . . .', but if the singer sings the same way several times, even a whole programme, the public is soon bored. The poet gives us so many pictures in so short a

time, *there* is our variety, and Debussy's music sings it for us. Let us keep their joy and life! Let your lips take life, rejoice and make your face animated.

(ii) La Grotte (Très lent, très doux)
I think that the rhythm, the sense of the phrase are so fully illuminated by this music, that I cannot share the opinion of those who find it sacrilege to set beautiful verses to music. In any case, for the interpreter, this joy of the words lifts him up with enthusiasm to serve the two artists. To serve them with all the mystery of our sonority, by the mysterious combination of intelligence and sensibility.

In this song the essential element is tenderness. No one word must take a foremost place, simply tenderness. Debussy's indications, *Très lent et très doux*, his markings of tempo and expression for voice and piano, tell us all we need to know.

(iii) Rondel: 'Pour ce que plaisance est morte'
Très modéré — and delicately expressive. This lovely, sad little lament must be sung simply, following Debussy's indications exactly. Each time 'Pour ce que plaisance est morte' comes, it is slower, as if he could not bear to let her go.

Le Promenoir des deux amants 1910 (poems: Tristan l'Hermite)
This work of Debussy's is infinitely tender and there is nothing to do but to sing what he has indicated. I have the impression that for this murmur between two lovers, even a small hall would be too large. The intimate quality must be created. I have heard Gieseking in the huge Salle Pleyel playing Debussy's works, and yet create just this for the listener by his way of not forcing, and, with an intimate framework, he produces an atmosphere that is attached to the slightest sound, 'suspendu'.

In the poems of the 'Promenoir' there must be this same kind of intimacy, but — and I insist — without this hardly perceptible 'nuance' being extinguished.

We must achieve in our interpretation a quality of silence, of which Maeterlinck speaks, that nothing can surpass. An interpreter must be equally capable of whispering as of vociferating.

(i) *La Grotte* see *Trois Chansons de France* (page 121)

(ii) *Crois mon conseil, chère Climène*

Très modéré and the piano 'softly expressive'. Addressing Climène, the first two bars of the voice part are flexible, a supple line.

In the *a tempo* the lover begs her to await the evening sitting with him by the fountain; *cédez* for two bars, then *au mouvement*. 'Does she not hear the sighing of the Zephyr?' *Cédez* for one bar, then *en animant et crescendo peu a peu*. 'The Zephyr too, seeing with wonder and love the roses on your cheek that are not in his kingdom?' After one bar, *a tempo* again, the bass of the piano slightly prominent. 'The Zephyr's mouth, full of perfume, has breathed on our path, mingling a spirit of jasmine with the' (*retenu* to the end) 'amber of your sweet breath.' And all the time the piano ebbs and flows with the fountain, rhythm of words and music perfectly united.

(iii) *Je tremble en voyant ton visage*

Rêveusement lent. The voice soft and very sustained in expression — piano *pp* 'constant', and marked 'supple' for the semi-quaver chords on the second page.

I think he is watching Climène's face mirrored in the water of the fountain's marble basin, and fears his sighs may wreck the reflection. 'Will she put him above all humans and let him drink the water from her cupped hands, if it does not melt the snow of her palms?'

The 'dé' of 'désirs' may be slightly longer, and the 'nau' of 'naufrage' a little more open in order to be able to round it in the curve of the phrase, not point it or accent it. If we follow the markings Debussy has made in tempo and nuances we shall do well.

Trois Ballades de François Villon 1910

(i) *Ballade de Villon à s'amie [s'amye]*

When Debussy returned to the fifteenth century and to François Villon, he created a wonderfully genuine mediaeval atmosphere with the direct, natural expression of this wild genius, in the most musically economical manner. On the first Ballade, 'From Villon to his love', Debussy writes, 'With an expression where there is as much anguish as regret'. The *triste et lent* of the accompaniment shows the heart sobbing, the lover lamenting, accusing his faithless beloved, and lamenting his helpless inability to escape from his bondage.

Watch the changes of tempo, and the accented articulation, that must be very clear in all these songs.

Then a great change: *Doux et mélancolique*, and the accompaniment perfectly mirrors the words foretelling the future of old age, when her flower of beauty will be withered, and he too old to laugh at her. 'Succour a poor man,' he says again. The ending is broader, a last appeal to love to have pity on him.

(ii) Ballade that Villon wrote at his mother's request as a prayer to Our Lady

This must not be sad. (I think a sad prayer must bore the good God.) Both poet and composer draw vivid pictures of this old woman, so ignorant she wants her son to write a fit prayer to the Virgin Mary for her. It must have simplicity and clarity. The music begins like a small hurdy-gurdy, *très modéré — doux et simple*.

In a religious ecstasy, the old woman praises the Queen of Heaven, and begs to be received (*cédez un peu*), 'me, your humble Christian' (*a tempo*) and be amongst your chosen, although I am not worth anything. She says, 'Your gracious gifts, my Lady Mistress, are far greater than my sins, without which many souls could not (*cédez*) merit the Heavens' (*a tempo*). 'I am not a liar.' The refrain (piously) 'In this Faith I want to live and die.'

Then a change of expression at 'Tell your Son I am His. May He take away my sins. Pardon me, as the Egyptian woman was forgiven' (*animant un peu*) and with increasing dramatic articulation: 'And as the clerk Theophilus was pardoned, in spite of his pact with the Devil — preserve me from ever doing such a thing!' (accented) 'Virgin, without any blasphemy may

I receive the Sacrament, celebrate in the Mass' (piously) 'In this Faith I want to live and die.' (Soft and humble) 'I am a poor, old woman, who knows nothing, and cannot read' (joyously) 'but at the Monastery, in my Parish, I see pictures of Paradise' (contrast) 'and of Hell where the damned are boiled! The one terrifies me, the other brings joy and rejoicing.' (Held back, softly and in ecstasy) 'The joy you have given me, supreme goddess; to you must all sinners go for aid, filled with Faith, with no doubts or sloth; in this Faith I want to live and die.'

(iii) Ballade des femmes de Paris

Debussy put 'Alert and gay'; and, above all, in this song we must observe and follow his indications exactly, *staccato*, *legato*, a strict tempo and rhythmic energy—noting his few markings, and the accents on words. Therefore the articulation must take first place. There are twenty-five different talkers and chatterers from different races, but none can compare with the women of Paris for their 'gift of the gab!'

The humour, and apparent search for even more comparisons, 'Have I named enough places?' must be expressed in the slight *retenu* and then, at the end, the Prince must give the prize to Paris (*a tempo*).

6. ALBERT ROUSSEL (1869–1937)

[At a class on his songs at the end of 1933 Roussel was present and played for some of the singers. Mme Croiza asked him to make some comments but he was reluctant to be critical, so Croiza took over and began by saying:] What I love about Roussel's music is its marvellous creative imagination [sa fantaisie merveilleuse], and its originality. When he is melancholy, he is melancholy, when he is joyful, he is joyful. The greatest fault I have to find with all the interpreters we have just heard is the lack of variety and lack of imagination and life.

[To a student]: 'Sarabande' and 'Le Jardin mouillé' will serve as absolutely typical examples. They are two very different works, but your interpretation of 'Sarabande' had the colour of

'Le Jardin mouillé', which is a melancholy song. I do not say either 'tragic' or 'sorrowful'. It has the same colour as 'Il pleure dans mon coeur'. It has the same character — melancholy, without drama — then, as often, the excessive sentiment of feminine interpretations! We must beware of excess in art, in life, in love, in friendship, in everything. And we must respect pauses, as useful in life as in music.

In 'Sarabande', then, I missed the aspect of animation and life that is there. If I were deaf and I looked at you, it would be impossible for me to guess, from your facial expression alone, the difference between the two songs you have sung.

Le Jardin mouillé (poem: Henri de Régnier)
Begin very evenly: if certain phrases are slowed up it is awkward for the pianist. Seek no sentimental effect. Sing it very simply, and give the quaver its full value. You are looking out at the garden, the sleeping garden; then leaf by leaf the rain wakes it, *plus animé* until the *poco ritenuto* on 'S'étire d'un geste engourdie'; then *a tempo* again, and a further *animez peu a peu* for six bars, and the *ritardando* on 'Comme d'imperceptibles pas' that must be lightly underlined by the diction. Roussel has these continual slight changes of tempo that are so perfectly in keeping with this lovely poem, the eyes raised in wonderment at 'L'averse semble maille à maille Tisser la terre avec le ciel'. A change of colour and a *rallentando* at the melancholy of self-realization once more.

Sarabande (poem: René Chalupt)
'Les jets d'eau dansent des sarabandes . . .' accentuate the 'd' of 'dansent', which must be dancing, light, intoxicated, not sad; 'Sur l'herbe parfumée des boulingrins; Il y a des rumeurs de soie dans le jardin, Et de mystérieuses présences.' Make the pictures the poet and the composer provide, see them, evoke them by the way you visualize them and think about them. 'Trois tourterelles se sont posées, Comme sur tes lèvres trois baisers . . .'. That is a declaration — the 'bai' in 'baisers' long . . . 'Car tu es nue sous ton manteau . . .' amorous.

Make it amorous by your articulation. Contrary to what I usually say about the mute 'e', it is absolutely necessary to pronounce the one in 'nue' to make it feminine; if it is in the masculine, it is absolutely indecent. 'Et c'est pour toi . . .' This is something ecstatic, not sad. And at the end, 'Viennent fleurir au bord de l'eau', there is an élan in both the words and music, full of movement and of freshness. Make 'this water's brim' something poetic. See it, look at it, look down at it, because unless it is the rain, water is below, not above!

When a singer who has a good 'key-board' allows himself a noble pronunciation of beautiful words, his career is assured.

A un jeune gentilhomme Opus 12 No. 1 (poem: H. P. Roché after the English translation by Professor Giles of a Chinese poem) Ode chinois
[Roussel observed:] The alternations in tempo between *mouvement* and *de retenue* must be respected, and the pauses in the same way.

[Croiza:] Imagination, variety and wit. I should not interfere on the musical side as the composer is here, but I shall be more severe than he about everything concerning precision, time etc. We must repeat a song, repeat it over and over again, until we are sure of every crotchet, and every quaver. . . . In 'A un jeune gentilhomme', as the composer has said, there is a double *mouvement* that goes forward and that holds back. There are also the three repetitions of 'Et même si je vous aime . . .' that must be different from one another, while paying attention to the *crescendo*. Here all is charm, irony, malice and again this *fantaisie* that is so French. Debussy said, 'Fantaisie dans la sensibilité' [Original, creative imagination within sensibility]. Give it all the sensibility, but do not take away its *fantaisie*. The girl's resistance diminishes. The variations are continuous.

Réponse d'une épouse sage Opus 35 No. 2 (poem: H. P. Roché as above)
Observe the changes of tempo. 'Tu m'as envoyé deux perles

précieuses', and Roussel wishes a complete change of expression at 'Et moi . . .', in spite of there being little to indicate this in the text.

'Avec les deux perles je te renvoie deux larmes . . .' but not tragic and certainly not 'Comédie Française', or, though she may regret him, he will certainly not regret her!

Amoureux séparés Opus 12 No. 2 (poem: H. P. Roché as above)
[Only a short note by the composer who said that in the phrase 'nuages sur vos fortes poitrines' one may very well make two crotchets instead of the triolet, otherwise it is too difficult to pronounce.]

Flammes Opus 10 (poem: G. Jean-Aubry)
[Roussel said:] The rhythm! It must move on! If the tempo is too slow, the rhythm is lost.

Nuit d'automne (poem: Henri de Régnier)
Every verse has its own different domain; there must be more variety. There is 'la mort grave et lente' but there is also 'le couchant large et beau . . .' Do not let us kill one by the other. I do not see anything in this text to justify sadness.

Jazz dans la nuit Opus 38 (poem: René Dommange)
This is a song full of humour, imagination and variety, and it has many pictures and moods. The scene is set for us by the composer and the poet. All these vital words 'irradiés — fous — étouffent — doux — fraise — s'évanouissent' — etc. . . . must be well articulated. It must be sung with a facial expression that reflects the slightly mocking tone, not sentimental. It must be full of *coquetterie*, and the ending must be *pianissimo*, voluptuous.

'Passant, ramasse ce mouchoir, tombé d'un sein tiède, ce soir.' . . . 'Il te livrera pour secret, le parfum d'une gorge nue . . .' Not too prudish, but subtly daring, the accentuation on 'gorge' not on 'nue'. 'Et la bouche d'une inconnue . . .' and let us hope that it will not be a tiresome stranger!

[After Roussel's death, Madame Roussel found some notes he had made for the interpretation of his works. 'Only for his symphonies,' she said. 'For the songs there is a tradition. Madame Croiza has created a tradition.' Croiza made recordings of Roussel's songs with the composer at the piano.]

7. MAURICE RAVEL (1875–1937)

Shéhérazade: Trois Poèmes de Tristan Klingsor 1903
  (i) Asie
  This poem is sensual, mysterious, cruel, amorous, a poem full of imagination and ardour. But what we make of it always lacks its Eastern and creative, imaginative character.
  The three 'Asie! Asie! Asie!' are always attacked too brutally. I see them as mysterious, and full of expectation and aspiration. Here is a poem to be put on the stage, and all the more because it is orchestrated! Bear-skins, an oriental interior, smoke, a sensual atmosphere, amorous, cruel, I repeat — 'Je voudrais m'en aller avec la goélette, Qui se berce ce soir dans le port mystérieux et solitaire'.
  Ravel indicates 'without taking a breath'. I have to say I find this terrible and not true to the 'breathing' in Klingsor's poem. I do not know why Ravel wanted it, but, speaking as an audacious interpreter, I think it is a mistake.
  'De beaux turbans de soie sur des visages noirs aux dents claires'. The importance is not in the 'd' of 'dents', but in a clarity that must light up everything. 'Je voudrais voir des cadis et des vizirs . . . qui, du seul mouvement de leur doigt. . . .'
  There is such elegance in the whole of this poem, and in Ravel's music, that it demands an aristocratic interpretation, full of nobility, without gestures. The song must not be interpreted like a queen of the theatre who loses her temper

and argues with her subjects, but like a true queen who commands. 'Les princesses aux mains fines . . .', very, very rhythmical. 'Et les lettrés qui se querellent . . .', also very rhythmical, with the accompaniment accented.

'Avec un personnage au milieu d'un verger . . .' Up to this point the interpretation remains quite light, but nevertheless without ever descending to an everyday level. What follows must be intensified without falling into vulgarity, which is the danger — 'Je voudrais voir des assassins . . .' — then the culminating point is attained in this vision, and in the singing, on a terrible high B flat. After this culminating point, there follows something calmer, I find once more an impression of the interior, of smoke, to the end. 'En élevant ma vieille tasse . . .'.

There is therefore a perfect curve, given in its wholeness in Ravel's music, passing through fantasy and ardour and returning gradually to simplicity, but to a regal simplicity.

(ii) La Flûte enchantée
The repulsive master, the charming slave-girl, here there is essentially a stage scene that can never be made clear enough by the interpreter. There are two characters with you, the horrid old man asleep in the alcove, and the delightful lover playing his flute to you outside in the street. So you are not alone beside a grand piano, not alone and sad.

Begin very softly — someone is asleep — you are walking on tip-toe so as not to awaken him. I always have the impression of a door being closed. Then the change, 'But I am still awake . . .' — let this 'moi', come out clearly, not like cotton-wool; 'and I am listening with rapture to the flute outside that my darling lover is playing for me . . . and as I approach the window it seems to me that every note is wafted to my cheek like a mysterious kiss'. The kiss must be exquisite and not sad, and 'mystérieux baiser' must be perfectly articulated. The more softly one sings, the more firmly one must articulate; make the 'bai' of 'baiser' a little longer. Your face must express your joy. The music must be exactly in place, and beware of the intonation of the last E, which is dangerous; at 'air langoureux', mentally stretch yourself languorously.

In all these works a little acting must be introduced (without movement, of course) as it immediately brings the characters alive.

(iii) L'Indifférent

Two things in opposition, again a scene to be acted mentally and interpreted by the vivid inner vision of this woman who opens her door for the attractive passer-by to come in. There is therefore this 'Entre'. And then he passes on — indifferent to her. So there must be eager waiting. Then the disillusionment of his passing her by and then disappearing from view until the end of the accompaniment.

Histoires naturelles 1906 (prose poems by Jules Renard)

These *Histoires naturelles* show a different side of nature, not so poetic perhaps but utterly natural — one may love them or not, but they are still gems of truth and humour, with hidden poetry of great beauty. They are prose poems, and in his settings of five of them Ravel took the novel decision of cutting off nearly all the final mute 'e's. He has characterized them perfectly and indicated everything for the interpreter.

(i) Le Paon

A wonderful scene, majestic, evocative, a sovereign bird quite unaware that he could be jilted.

(ii) Le Grillon

A wonderful little vignette of this tiny creature putting his house in order, winding up his watch, shutting his door and turning the key — but still feeling unsafe he burrows down into the earth; at the end, 'Dans la campagne muette les peupliers se dressent comme des doigts en l'air et désignent la lune.' After the crisp diction relating his activities, this ending must bring poetry and a perfect *legato*.

(iii) Le Cygne

A perfect picture in words and music of the swan gliding over the water 'like a white sledge' — trying to catch the reflections of the clouds in the clear water. Perhaps he will die from this illusion, but no! every time he plunges his long neck he brings up a worm. He is getting as fat as a goose. Very poetic and must be very *legato* — then the complete contrast, spoken after 'Qu'est ce que je dis . . .' and using facial mime.

(iv) Le Martin-pêcheur
'Ça n'a pas mordu ce soir . . .' not too poetic, not too serious. Begin very simply as though speaking. Then, at 'mais je rapporte une rare émotion', confide all the poetry in this experience. Note that 'peur' must be open. It is difficult, but there must be a distinct difference made between the 'eu' open and the 'eu' closed, for example, un oeuf — open — and des oeufs — closed.

(v) La Pintade
This needs a harsh, very clearly articulated interpretation. It is a vivid picture in words and music of a quarrelsome, frenzied, hump-backed guinea-fowl, with her piercing dis-cordant cry, laying her eggs in a field, and returning to roll in the dust of the farm-yard.

From *L'Enfant et les sortilèges 1925 (Colette)*
Air de l'Enfant
This exquisite, simple and lyrical little song, sung by the child after the beautiful princess is dragged away, must be begun *pianissimo*, and do not let the notes of the beginning overlap each other, no pedal effect, not pointed but *legato*. Do not hurry; it must be very 'balanced'.

After the *pianissimo* phrases comes a *piano* at 'Tu m'as laissé comme un rayon de lune' but do not start with a *crescendo*, keep the tempo and the tenderness. After 'qu'un cheveu d'or sur mon épaule' sing *più piano*, at 'un cheveu d'or, and *pp* for 'et les débris d'un rêve . . .'. Do not let 'rêve' arrive too soon, hold it back very slightly. And in pronouncing 'rêve', give the 'rê' its right length, do not sing a 'rêve' where the 've' is accentuated.

Mélodies populaires grecques 1904–06
(i) Chanson de la mariée
[Mme Croiza stressed the rhythm of all these folk songs, so

clearly expressed by Ravel, and the need to study his exact indications and sing them without rigidity, or losing the 'folk' character.] By the articulation, help the variety for this song with its joyful 'family' feeling.

(ii) Là-bas, vers l'église

Here a complete contrast must be made, starting *pp*, as if a procession, far away, draws nearer to this ancient church where numberless heroes of the past and present are reunited. Again, Ravel's indications tell us exactly what he wanted, providing a supple, almost hypnotic rhythm.

(iii) Quel galant m'est comparable!

A man's song, rather than a woman's, with a demanding rhythm, *forte* until the last 'Et c'est toi que j'aime!' which should be sung with great tenderness and a quiet *rallentando*.

(iv) Chanson des cueilleuses de lentisques

This song, sung by the women in the fields, slow, with an undulating rhythm and long phrases, is very Byzantine in character. The tune must sound very old, as if sung almost unconsciously, and yet the words are both personal and universal.

(v) Tout gai!

Vary the 'la la la's'! Again, the dancing rhythm must be very exact. The piano part, marked *pp*, should be undeviating in rhythm until the last three bars of the voice part where, after a pause in the first, the second is *rallentando* and the third *a tempo*.

8. André Caplet (1878–1925)

What are special in Caplet's music are the *tempi*. There is always one part that moves on and one part that holds back. There are hardly ever two or three bars in succession that are in identical tempo. Caplet is the opposite to Fauré in this respect, for the latter writes *a tempo* at the beginning and does not change from it.

Caplet, we must always remember, came from Normandy — and characteristically in order to be slow, 'it is not slow', and in order to be fast, 'it is not fast'. Always there is some juggling in the music, but also a touching sensibility on which any interpretation of his music must be based. So be sure to establish a plan, a frame and characters. Like Toscanini, Caplet respects the 'plan' of sonorities.

Forêt (poem: Rémy de Gourmont)
For me, Caplet's 'Forêt' has an emotional quality and an inner richness that are unique.

Speaking last year about *Orphée*, I mentioned the difference between the scene of the action of a work, the action itself, and the characters. All that forms the frame. But nature must be enlarged by us as interpreters. In 'Forêt' the marvellous vision of the opening should be quite different from what comes after the pause. 'Toi qui vis passer . . .'; the pause mark after the first 'O forêt' does not appear in the printed copy, but Caplet wanted a pause here. It is needed in order to separate the call from that which follows, which is something living, not something melancholy. For there is a marked contrast in the music, as in Gourmont's poem, between the forest itself and the characters it sees passing by.

Caplet's characters are always living, human beings. I did not know Caplet when he wrote 'Forêt', but my instinct follows his notation absolutely where he indicates 'sans lenteur', each time immediately after the 'O forêt', before the introduction of his characters.

The second time there is a *ritardando* followed by the quicker tempo for 'Souviens-toi de ceux qui sont venus un jour d'été . . .', a summer, not an autumn day.

When Caplet was accompanying and came to the three phrases, 'couleur de feuilles, couleur d'écorces, couleur de rêves' he coloured the first two, 'Une pichenaude sur une coupe de crystal [A flick on a crystal goblet]'. But at the third he returned to the low register and slower tempo for the first bar. These three colours must all be different and alive. Seize, in interpretation, on that gleam of joy that passes in less than a second ['un millième de fil'], seize on it — communicate it by the expression of your face. Without that we fall into monotony and declamation.

When Caplet returns to Nature, he finds expansive joy again [épanouissement], as in 'le bout du monde' in Duparc's 'L'Invitation au voyage'. Nature cannot be expressed here by force, but only by the intensity of the inner vision.

So, a *ritardando* at the third 'O forêt' and then back again to the quicker tempo for 'Tu fus bonne, en laissant le désir fleurir, au sein de ta verdure'. 'Fleurir' is marked *piano* but in spite of the respect we owe the composer, we need not respect this too literally. Caplet wrote it thus originally, it is true, but afterwards he did not observe it himself. Then comes the fourth 'O forêt', and 'Ceux qui sont venus fouler tes herbes solitaires et contempler (distraits) tes arbres ingénus'. Caplet's parentheses are very much his own and always Norman. And finally the beautiful *plus lent et rall* at 'et le pâle océan de tes vertes fougères' — *perdendosi* in the accompaniment.

Prières

The two first are prayers for oneself alone. Everyone can sing them; they are prayers for every day. But 'Prière normande' is a prayer for a crowd and demands a large voice. It must be made an affirmation that is beyond discussion. Even the most *pianissimo* nuances in this prayer remain superhuman, they stay on the level of total and complete affirmation, of a faith that must lead crowds to believe.

In 'Prière normande' there are necessary changes of tempo, and I stress them because they are contrary to what I generally say. In this prayer there is a note of familiarity, and a note of respect that must appear simultaneously, and this is a challenge to the imagination. Half respectful, half humorous, this is typically Norman — the prayer of two typical Normans! 'For a year when there are apples, there are no apples, for a year when there are no apples there are apples!' The humorous side is incontestable, and also the fervour.

'Seigneur Dieu de toute chose' — very, very forward moving and beneath all the rest, this French-peasant character of the text, this peasant who wants masses of flowers, lots of fruit, a lot of everything — even if there is too much, even if it must rot in the granary; this typical peasant who finds it so good to have a lot, and who never has too much.

'Prière: "Notre Père" . . .' [The Lord's Prayer]. A prayer is not a poem but something interior. The more intimate you make it the better it will be. This setting must be sung, not for the audience, but for oneself. And not too 'vécu', not too emotional, but as a prayer for every day.

Oraison dominicale
[To a student:] The only fault that I find in your singing of this, if I may say so, is that you were not alone with God — we were all too important to you so that the character of prayer was lost.

Quand reverrai-je? (poem: du Bellay)
Caplet wrote above this song, 'Some verses by du Bellay describing a state of the soul'. It seems to me that the composer found exactly the right rhythm for this little poem. If we do not distort the music but sing it faithfully, giving the poem its true form and meaning, we should arrive at a perfect interpretation.

Sonnet de Pierre de Ronsard
'Doux fut le trait':
Everyone knows my love of both consonants and vowels. I have no favourites because it depends on the word, but I must say that the 'D' seems to me particularly expressive. This poem could serve as a game with the 'd's continuously appearing, as in 'doux', 'doucement', 'doucettement', 'douce', and they must all be brought out, and I see that the composer accentuates these 'd's a little more each time.

This poem is a cameo of 'd's. How do you think we can express Ronsard's idea if we are not aware of these thousand deliberately planned details? 'Travail du travail', says Valéry.

Caplet understood these nuances, and he has made admirable play with them. 'Cette douceur si doucement douce', what enchantment in Caplet's line here!

We, who knew Caplet, know how much store he put on plays of sonority. In music everything depends on quality of sound. Music is not noise. Whatever may be true of composers, we interpreters must think first of the sonorous quality of our instrument: think music and not noise. The 'matter' of the sound and the sonorous 'matter' of the words — that is what the interpreter should seek above everything.

Caplet also had an extraordinarily sonorous speaking voice. One day, I remarked on it and he replied, 'I fabricated it for myself, because I could not bear not being heard by the orchestra.'

La Ronde (poem: Paul Fort)

'La Ronde' is one of the most difficult of Caplet's songs, one of those of which I am never sure until I have finished singing. Caplet always used to say, 'les tabliers qui volent', very rhythmical! [Mme Croiza tapped her heels and clicked her fingers in the rhythm.] It is one of these modern songs in which the composer wants an understanding of the text to predominate, without realizing the difficulty of achieving this on awkward notes.

This reminds me of an anecdote. Yvette Guilbert came to my flat one morning to meet Caplet, whom she wished to know. I was imprudent enough to ask her how she would sing this final passage of 'La Ronde'. She managed the words perfectly, but as to getting back on to a G — it proved impossible, and she said so! Caplet was not best pleased, but there is no way of saving both the word and the note if the two are incompatible. It is too nerve-racking, and the composer makes it too difficult for an interpreter anxious to save the word. In modern music it is like this all the time — one is asked to articulate at pitches that simply do not allow articulation. Such music demands, before any interpretation, musical precision that can manage absolutely anything; and Caplet understood that perfectly. He had a habit of striking, with all ten fingers at once, ten notes on the key-board, and then saying, 'Sing me the G, the B etc.'.

L'Adieu en barque (poem: Paul Fort)
A song that is full of poetry and the call of the night. The difficulty is that it is so bare [dépouillé] that we can do nothing but try not to disturb the atmosphere. We cannot add anything. [To a student:] 'Vers le ciel bleu . . .' You did not express the winged flight, the curve, the soaring. It is always said that the great artists are those who feel the most nervous tension or emotion. But Mme Olénine d'Alheim feared nothing, she did not think about the public, nor anything else; she only thought of the musician.

I have the impression that we interpreters never look sufficiently exactly at what composers have written. We are inaccurate, and confuse nuance, tempo and expression. The interpreters of the Romantics certainly had the right to be freer in their interpretations than we who sing Ravel and Debussy. We must pay attention to the slightest detail, as everything is noted. But in practising we must also use our musical instinct — if we have one! Do not let reflection and instinct try to influence each other; each should obey its own law.

[Caplet's great religious work, *Le Miroir de Jésus — Mystères du rosaire* (Henri Ghéon), was dedicated to Mme Croiza who gave the first performance in 1924.]

9. DARIUS MILHAUD (1892–1974)

It is more difficult for me to talk today than on other days. My task is not easy because (and I am going to make a comparison with painting) I have the impression that in a museum, pictures which have come to be generally accepted are no longer under discussion. In our museum, however, in this series of song-writers, we bring and hang up a canvas which is still being discussed. Some say, 'It is impossible'; others, 'It is admirable'. And agreement is very hard to come by.

We have just been listening to the *Poèmes juifs* of Darius Milhaud. If we listened without prejudice, relaxed, with a listener's relaxation that is at least as necessary as that of the interpreter, we cannot deny their strength, their beauty, their sincere enthusiasm.

These are very difficult works, works in which one is always anxious whilst singing, and never sure of having sung correctly, even if they have been studied very carefully . . .

The last part of the 'Chant du laboureur' is a kind of trumpet-call of victory. I think that modern composers who wish to strike up this trumpet of victory, do not always use the part of the voice that can give it to them. There is a misunderstanding of the voice, of the instrumental voice, of its 'tessitural capacity'.

In these songs we must look for means of expression in all that is not properly called 'voice'. I think of Mme Olénine, and of the radiance she had in singing these songs with a voice without richness, but with such an intensity of expression that the means disappeared. I heard her sing these 'Poèmes juifs' after some Mussorgsky, and the unification was complete. It was absolute, a kind of 'Victoire de Samothrace'.

Mme Lalo, Charles Lalo's wife, always spoke of the difficulty she had had to 'impose' Schubert and Schumann on her public. She was reproached for singing impossible composers! Every epoch brings a renewed perspective [optique renovée] of strangeness. We well know, those of us who have had a career partly in the theatre [opera house], that fashion brings its tastes and imposes them. Even in *Carmen*, even in *Werther*, a wardrobe designer in Spain, 'arranges' Alsace. He lengthens or shortens the skirts, makes small or large hats. I have sung Charlotte (*Werther*) in a hat that, today, would have apples thrown at it. I was Charlotte just the same. But every epoch imposes a reassessment, an accommodation of the eye.

There is also an accommodation of the ear. *Pelléas* was a

revolution, a turning 'upside-down' [une bousculade] of everything that had been sung until then, of everything that one had been accustomed to hear. I remember Mme Gounod, then very old, declaring at the exit, that it was impossible. . . .

But I reproach modern composers for their disregard of the voice, and I regret that they write for it without being in love with it. They do not love the voices they handle. I have just been reading Pierre Lalo's book on Wagner. Lalo says that one of the things that struck Wagner most forcibly, and chiefly influenced his musical direction, was hearing Mme Schroeder-Devrient in *Fidelio*. Well, I do not see, at the present time, a modern composer returning home with a revelation of this sort.

[Croiza also quoted Ravel's reply to an enquiry by the journal, *Excelsior*, about his opinion of composers under twenty-five years of age, and how he seemed to expect more of them than of those aged forty. Ravel replied: 'They separate themselves clearly from the troop of pioneers and sappers who preceded them. They are much more preoccupied to learn their profession than they were to take pains with their writing. They no longer make music with blows. They work harder than their immediate elders, produce less, and find their way more and more towards a sort of rather curious neo-classicism. It is still very difficult to divine the mysterious objects towards which their instinct directs them. One can, however, recognize in their works a care for clarity, for purity and frankness, a love of life and of light, and a kind of inward light-heartedness whose generosity has much merit. One does not find in them any prejudiced writing.' And Croiza said: 'May what he says be true. If there existed somewhere an unknown composer who would be willing to listen to me, I would conjure him to learn the laws of the human voice before writing for it. To learn about the tessituras, the ease and difficulties of articulation, and how necessary it is to write in tessituras that allow the poems to be "respected" as they themselves want them to be.

'I wish above all for the composers of the future, a little

more musical culture, and a little more love of the voice, this instrument that is so noble, so beautiful, the most beautiful of all because it is the only living one. In their own interest may composers understand the voice and keep for it, in music, the rôle for which it is made.']

[Claire Croiza's involvement in, and admiration for Darius Milhaud's magnificent and powerful *Choéphores* must be mentioned here. Milhaud set Claudel's translation of Aeschylus' *The Oresteia* — *II*; and the excerpts, Exhortation and Conclusion, from it were recorded by Columbia in the astonishing performance by Louis de Vocht and the Chorale Caecilia d'Anvers with the Société des Nouveaux Concerts of Antwerp and Claire Croiza declaiming the solo, Choéphore. The poet, Valéry, receiving the record in America, wrote to Croiza saying what a marvel it was to be able to hold her captive as the suppliant Choéphore if one had the desire of 'poetic exaltation', and 'the immediate response' of a voice that 'exhorts and invokes with sacred violence "le Père Zeus de tous les Olympiens". Then the rhythmic tumult of a mystical and furious uprising bursts out, an invisible, vehement mob supports, submerges and uncovers your noble vociferation.' . . . 'It seized and transported us when you gave us with all your enthusiastic soul, this voice of the suppliant Choéphore that abjures, and, menacing, demands . . .']

NINE

THE INTERPRETER ON STAGE

IN THE OPERATIC work we are doing here, my ambition would be for everybody to find themselves, to release their true nature and to gain confidence in it.

In the opera house, there is the opera itself. Why do singers, who are going to tackle a rôle, not work at it with a talented actor? Once the music is learnt, it must be acted. An actor would provide a correcting influence and a focus. But before doing any acting, the singer must know the rôle, and know it like an old story; and if he does not start from an absolutely exact musical foundation, and one that is absolutely sure, he cannot do anything.

The longer I live, the more I am persuaded that what counts most in opera is the personality of the interpreter. He depends on the truth within himself to express the truth of the characters. During the stage rehearsals it would sometimes be better to leave certain things badly done, within the interpreter's personality, rather than try to rectify them and, in so doing, make him lose it. When an actor has some personality, do not let us massacre it in advance by covering it up with convention, let us let it live.

The principal fault of the opera house today is that there is no life in it.

Accustom yourself to salvage the mistakes you make. If by mistake you drop your handkerchief, well, pick it up, instead of pushing it away with your foot, looking as if you did not see it! Pick it up, continuing to act naturally, incorporating it into your rôle. You have a shawl? Wrap yourself in it, or wrap it round you. You have a handkerchief? Weep. Behave as you would in everyday life. True theatre is the monologue of the rôle while life continues. In what Lucien Guitry did, the manner in which he rolled a cigarette had as much importance as what he said while rolling it.

On the stage, one has no right to have accidents — one must always know, or foresee any obstacles and, in any case, try to avoid them. If you are motionless before singing, remain still for a moment when you begin to sing. If you begin to move at once, it looks artificial. Likewise, if you are walking on the stage before singing, do not stop walking, but sing whilst walking; otherwise it becomes theatrical and unreal. When you are holding on to a chair, or a piece of furniture on stage, do not be too far away, do not lean on it at arms' length. Whatever you do, try to be natural.

One always imagines that one can only work if one is with someone else, but this is not true. It is when one is face to face with oneself that one works best; this work of the inner life is to seek the character, the state of the soul, trying to live it, to create it. Work at your rôles by living them. Work at your scenes in your own room. Learn to be alive, learn to come in, learn to go out. Afterwards, if a producer makes you enter here or there, if he places you on the right, or on the left, it does not matter for you will know how to enter or exit, and how to hold yourself, because you will know how to live. I have never attached absolute importance to being told: 'look here', 'look there . . .'; of what importance is it so long as you look as if you were seeing something? Everything is in that.

The art of the actor is to resemble everyday life as nearly as he can. The greatest actor is the one who succeeds in giving a type of character by simplifying it as much as possible. It is the greatest compliment one can pay an interpreter to say: 'He does nothing, and that is it!' For me, he is the true interpreter.

In all acting we must get as close to the truth as possible. Make 'guide-marks' in the action, like the train that must pass a station at such and such a time, and at another station at another time. Fix three or four 'guide-marks' for yourself to accord with the music, on which to fall exactly. But between these 'guide-marks' do not become too much a slave of the production and the indications — *live!*

An exclamation! A cry! A tragedian can put it where he pleases. For us singers, one of the most terrible necessities is that the cry must fall on the note. However, this cry must come from your own nature, from your own human self.

So long as an artist, on the stage, looks round at the public, he cannot be 'in' his stage character. From your first scene, accustom yourself to having a 'straight' look. Here again, take a 'guide-mark' in front of your eyes. Apart from a mystical rôle, make it a habit to keep your glance horizontal. Lower the eyes when it is necessary, but never lower the head.

Authority comes largely from immobility. One must learn to act with this immobility, but with the soul and the face of the character of course. Our Lyric Theatre is 'undone' by the gestures, by disorderly running about the stage, by useless agitation. We act badly because we move too much. We must not move more on the stage than in real life. On the contrary, we can move less because, in the theatre, everything is a mirage and it needs very little to give the illusion of reality. The face must give much, and the body little. Do not make too many gestures, or gestures that are too rapid or meaningless. That is your business and your sensibility as an artist. But whatever your choice may be, let your gesture be appropriate and may it be slow. Let it last as long as the phrase you are pronouncing.

Decide on your gestures, settle your immobility, and decide all this beforehand. Whatever your gesture may be, whatever your expression may be, hold yourself with assurance, according to your natural posture. All soldiers learn to stand upright in front of the General and they hold themselves straight, even to the last peasant. Therefore everything can be learnt, and there is a disciplined carriage to be acquired and kept. Provided the line of intention is there, the gestures are unimportant. The fewer you make the better. The more inwardly alive and yet motionless your character becomes, the more intense he will be. Never let the gesture precede the 'réplique'. This is one of the worst errors on the stage. Walk, or stay still; whether in opera or on the concert platform, never make a movement for no reason. Avoid 'little steps', fidgeting and vacillation on stage. In tragedy, you must have an ample gait, even on a very small stage, where one must succeed in creating the illusion of space, or the character will be let down.

When you are addressing yourself to someone, let it be truly to him you are speaking. Let there be a bond from you to him, a gesture, a look or even, simply, conviction to establish this bond.

On the stage the actor who is not acting at that moment, must always help the actor who is speaking, or acting. Never put your partner in the position of playing with his back to the public. Never speak in front of your partner, never be obliged to move backwards in order to find the tenor! When we make a mistake it is never the other's fault, it is our own. We can never know our rôle well enough — it is not sufficient to know it well, it must be known too well. And do not count on another's help, do everything without relying on him. Always think his entry may be late, or the curtain may be slow in falling: let your character continue to live beyond his 'réplique' [response], beyond his aria. Provided that your mind is entirely concentrated on what you are doing, provided that your face is full of expression, provided that your body is held upright with balanced lines, provided that your expression lives, then you can give no matter which work, no matter what opera, almost without moving, almost without gestures.

At the Monnaie I often listened to singers' auditions — everyone knows the aria in Massenet's *Werther*, 'Les Larmes', that lasts scarcely two pages. Well, one day I counted the same arm gesture made seventeen times by a particular singer. I said to myself, 'If only this unfortunate singer had not moved, how much she would have impressed the directors'. The physiognomy, this magnificent thing: eyes, a mouth . . . an actor can act with his body, with his features, but his 'look'? Mary Garden had a rather wild, savage look, but with a sureness: a look that did not hesitate. Hesitation on the stage is always worthless — project energy! We must forget ourselves, but clothe the character with vigour, not let our own nature 'occupy the whole apartment'. We seldom go to the complete extent of what we could do with confidence, reflection and will-power.

The superiority of doing operatic work, as I see it from long experience, is that it frees us from nearly all our shackles on the concert platform, where it is hard to have real superiority if one has not passed through stage experience. In opera, the conductor insists on our singing in time, but we are also obliged to do other things, to think about other things. At a concert, it is more difficult to escape from a purely musical atmosphere and gain the necessary relaxation to interpret freely.

1. Orphée in Gluck's opera

It is inadvisable to sing this rôle too young.

Act I
It seems to me that the art of recitative is being lost. In the first place, recitatives are taken too slowly and the pauses are neglected. A recitative is the explanation of a situation, the link between an action and an aria and it must have life, life and still more life! All this is explained by the words.

The recitatives of Act I are perhaps the most difficult in the whole work because of their *tessitura*. They were transposed for Mme Viardot from the original, which was written for a castrato singer, and this often falsified the sonority of the cry 'Eurydice, Eurydice!' so that what one cannot, and must not try to give by volume, must be expressed by the vocal colour, by the articulation of the words and the intensity of feeling. Gluck maintains a dramatic curve throughout these recitatives with incomparable skill, but I am always struck by the small difference that singers make between the words they pronounce. Articulation must be the foundation of these recitatives.

'Vos plaintes, vos regrets . . .' is addressed by Orphée to the sympathetic crowd around the tomb of Eurydice. He then asks the crowd to leave him to mourn alone. 'Eurydice, Eurydice, ombre chère . . .': Besides his grief, we must also express Orphée's virility and his tenderness, otherwise it is incomplete and monotonous. He is a splendid Being, who cries aloud his love to the gods, to Nature and to Eurydice herself; and in these next two recitatives there are thus three elements to vary. 'Ces bois, ces rochers, ce vallon . . .': When you have the good fortune to have Nature as the framework and as an element, express her, and express her grandeur and vastness. Nature, that takes us out of our poor 'self' — the vastness of Nature that is there like an atmosphere. And there, too, is something human and something divine in this frame for Orphée. Let us express both, bring both alive — this life that is the source of all expression. 'Je lis ce mot gravé par une main tremblante. . . .' Start *piano*. Orphée is terrifying to sing for a sensitive interpreter who is not contented merely with the voice. 'Dieux, rendez-lui la vie, ou donnez-moi la mort . . .': We must communicate this by the intensity of our own feeling from within, without forcing the voice.

'Divinités de l'Acheron . . .': If we start this recitative *fortissimo* where shall we go? It must be 'attacked' in such a way that we can make a gradual *crescendo*, progressively, while dramatic intensity must be attained by the expression and articulation, not simply by vocal volume. At 'La beauté, la jeunesse . . . n'a plus la garantir?' there must be an illumination, through the memory of her grace and her youth until 'implacables tyrans . . .', where there is a sharp contrast, and 'Je me sens assez de courage . . .' gives us the virile Orphée, the Orphée who has made his decision, that we have not seen before.

Then comes Cupid's aria, like a refreshing breeze in this drama, and 'Dieux! je la reverrais!' Orphée is triumphant, already happy. . . .' 'A tout mon âme est preparée!' Cupid's recitatives and aria warn Orphée of the terrible conditions laid down by the gods for his leading Eurydice back to Earth, and Life, and Orphée's recitative at the end of this act is full of contrasts and quick changes of feeling. 'Qu'entends-je? . . . Eurydice, vivra! . . . Mais quoi! Je ne pourrai . . . quelle faveur, et quel ordre inhumain . . .' a flame of joy and an ice-cold fear — breaking the ice with red-hot irons — and Gluck's rhythm underlines it perfectly. 'Douter de ton bienfait serait te faire injure. C'en est fait, dieux puissants, j'accepte votre loi' — and Orphée goes off triumphant after singing the aria, 'Amour, viens rendre à mon âme. . . .' Once again, remember that he must be interpreted not only as grief-stricken but sensitive and virile, and god-like.

Act II, Scene I

In the first scene, the Furies in Hell, it is no harder to pluck the strings of the lyre in time than against, on 'Laissez-vous toucher par mes pleurs . . .' It only needs a little practice. Work at this aria first as a vocalise. Resist the temptation to sing 'Laissez-vous toucher' fast and 'La tendresse qui me presse . . .' slower and slower; there should be no *rallentando*, on the contrary, Orphée becomes increasingly urgent and the tempo quickens.

Sing 'Laissez-vous toucher . . .' in *bel canto* style. The singing tone comes before everything, for this is no longer a recitative but an aria. Once again, practise the aria first as a vocalise before putting in the words. Add the words only after placing the aria on vowels, vocalizing it.

Act II, Scene 2: The Elysian Fields

After Eurydice sings with the chorus, it is the custom for Orphée to arrive without his lyre. Why? Simply because he wants to be able to make large gestures. I maintain that Orphée must have his lyre in this scene. One hand is enough for him to lead Eurydice, and it is much more beautiful for him to hold this symbolic lyre, that has been part of his image from the beginning. The aria, 'Quel nouveau ciel pare ces lieux . . .' should be sung in almost total silence, should scarcely make the atmosphere vibrate. It is a stupefying contrast after the infernal regions! And although I detest *rallentandi*, take your time here, create silences. The orchestra makes this possible by often keeping silent. Do not forget that gestures upset such poetic, paradisical scenes, and that a look is enough to give the expression. There are many different colours in this aria. The pause which precedes the entry of the voice must be a long silence, very marked. Then begin softly, very well articulated, but with no colour, slow and as if in Paradise — Orphée is dazzled. 'Quel nouveau ciel . . . Quels sons harmonieux . . .' in an easy tempo, without dragging (Do not forget the birds are in the trees — 'du ramage des oiseaux' — and the streams on the earth — 'du murmure des ruisseaux . . . et des soupirs de zéphire . . .'). It is difficult to sing this aria away from the stage, for which it was written. But if one is faithful to the written notes, everything is created by the precision and purity of Gluck's music. 'On goute en ce séjour un éternel repos.' Here is the summit of this atmosphere of Paradise, so we may give more voice, with a *diminuendo* on 'repos'.

But after this, disquiet returns, something new, tormented, that we must make felt. 'Mais le calme qu'on y respire, ne saurait adoucir, mes maux.' Differences of expression become obvious if we work at the words only, without singing. Orphée's uneasiness, make 'O toi, doux objet de ma flamme, les accents tendres et touchants . . .' tender, 'sont les seuls biens que je désire . . .' not loud, but lengthen 'désire'. His anxiety persists until the off-stage chorus, 'Le destin répond à tes voeux . . .', renews his hope and expectation.

All this scene finds expression in the singer's inward vision. It is not the painted scenery that inspires him, but his own vision and the music, and his sinking himself in the words, and the poetry and Nature that they express, and all this he must rediscover within himself.

Act III

The gods allow Orphée to rescue Eurydice only if he does not

look at her, or clasp her in his arms on their way. The rôle of
Eurydice is wrongly considered unrewarding. I have always
thought Mme Caron would have made a wonderful Eurydice, with her 'glance', her 'look'. For my part, I have never
seen a Eurydice who has satisfied me. That is to say, I have
never seen one who has sung the rôle with conviction, saying
to herself, 'How beautiful it is!'

For me, these recitatives of Orphée and Eurydice at the
beginning of Act III have the typical tempo of recitative.
Orphée is all urgency, joy and rapture at finding Eurydice; her
answering joy is such that she can hardly believe in it.

But at 'mais par ta main, ma main n'est plus pressée . . .'
there is a change. Eurydice cannot accept that Orphée will
not look at her; and he, obliged to obey the gods' agonizing
decree until they are safely away from Hades, tries in vain to
hasten their steps and to reassure her. She asks why he will
not even look at her, and this situation continues through
their duet, her recitative and aria and their second duet and
final recitative, at the end of which, Orphée, driven to
desperation by Eurydice's suspicions and accusations, turns
to her with all his pent-up tenderness; and as he looks at her,
she falters and dies.

Here there must be a pause of horror and incredulous
despair, a silence that can express more than any words —
whereas, as a rule, the chord is hardly sounded before the
recitative is begun. 'Malheureux, qu'ai-je fait?' We must
respect the movement of the words, the rests, the pauses and
the anguish, and give them live significance.

Of the aria, 'J'ai perdu mon Eurydice', it could be said that
when a dramatic aria has three stanzas that are repeated with
the same words and the same music, it is up to the interpreter
to vary the expression and the dynamics. One feels very
strongly in this aria that the culminating stanza is the last one,
the climax of Orphée's anguish and despair. When an
interpreter has to vary stanzas like these, she must be very sure
of the culminating point, and construct everything in relation
to it.

So, the first stanza should be stupefied, immobile, frozen. And at the appeal, 'Eurydice . . . réponds-moi. . . . C'est ton époux . . .', an infinite tenderness — leading into the second stanza, *pianissimo*, despair turned in on itself, almost murmured, as if you had her beloved head in your hands. Keep this intimate tender voice for the second 'j'ai perdu' refrain.

Then he turns elsewhere, 'Eurydice! Eurydice!' he cries, and listens. No reply. 'Mortel silence! Vaine espérance! Quelle souffrance déchire mon coeur!', and the appeal becomes a cry, a *crescendo* of mounting torment, of the re-awakening of his whole being to his suffering, leading into the third stanza with no pause, sung full out to the *fortissimo* climax and *affetuoso* until the last 'a' of 'ma douleur' which is lengthened a little.

I must insist again on the need for an expressive facial mime. Think of the character, live inside it, let your facial expression communicate it. The more vocal powers singers have, the less they think of the character, and of their expression. But if the voice is not accompanied by all that makes an artist, the most beautiful tones become monotonous. In Orphée we are borne on by love, by hope, by Nature. It is drama with a continual rebound. Our interpretation must be truthful, the true expression that we should give to our own grief and joy, magnified in order to reach the listener, not in volume but in expression.

To sum up, if it be in *Alceste*, in *Orphée*, in *Iphigénie*, one kills the characters under the pretext they are classic, and therefore must be made cold. But, on the contrary, it is Life that must be given to them by the force of feeling, expression, greatness. To be able to do this, everything must be living very strongly within us. When the 'being' is not there, when the interpretation of the character is incomplete, when there is nothing behind the façade, I often find myself thinking, 'Oh, unaccompanied baggage'. To create a character, it helps to think of a living type, a great artist, actor, interpreter, and fill this mould with our own feeling and intelligence.

2. CARMEN IN BIZET'S OPERA, WITH REFERENCE TO MÉRIMÉE

I am going to try and tell you what I think of Carmen from the point of view of the interpreter. This rôle is one of the most difficult — for a number of reasons.

Chief of these reasons is, I think, the fact that the character in the libretto is a distortion of Mérimée's original. The libretto, as such, is a masterpiece, but the false theatricality of the 1870s has distorted the original and the whole rôle of Micaela was added to satisfy the exigencies of the day. No opera could be conceived without a soprano coming on to sing her big aria. I often heard Mme Gounod relate how, in order to have Mme Carvalho for his interpreter, Gounod was obliged to introduce a waltz into all his operas — whether *Faust* or *Mireille* — if one wanted Mme Carvalho there must be a waltz, there must be a big aria. At the time of *Carmen* this convention had to be respected (whether it was legitimate or not is another matter), just as there had to be a Micaela arriving with her fair plaits among the cigarette girls and the gypsies!

The first conflict, then, for the singer who turns to Mérimée for the character of the rôle is that his is not the same character. Mérimée belongs to her own world, while the Carmen of Meilhac and Halévy belongs — for better or for worse — to the Opéra-Comique. Their Carmen is not a true gypsy.

I seem to be beginning at the end, but I feel that Carmen is grossly misrepresented in her death scene. Mérimée's Carmen has indeed loved Jose but she no longer cares for him: Jose leads her to her death, but she does not care, she has no fear. She is resolute, full of virile courage. In Meilhac and Halévy, at Don Jose's first reproach, Carmen is frightened, she may tap her foot, she may throw his ring in his face, but she has no longer any virile courage. The libretto makes her run from side to side on the stage, and smothers her dying in false tragedy.

The first problem for an interpreter, then, is that the story has been falsified by the libretto. The second, is that the rôle of Carmen demands a consummate actress; but the gift of a voice may be anyone's. The singer who can sing the part is the singer chosen. Whether or not she can act the rôle is not considered, although there must — above all in Carmen — be a union of the singer and the actress. The third difficulty is the rhythm. And here the question of race enters. Carmen is a gypsy. We have seen real gypsies in music halls, apparently motionless, but their whole bodies forming an invitation by means of an imperceptible rhythm, an undulation. Most French operatic Carmens lack rhythm, they dance too much and achieve nothing.

In saying that Carmen is a difficult rôle, I am aware that easy rôles and difficult rôles are perhaps not what the public thinks. I judge that if a large number of interpreters have played it badly, a rôle is difficult. When I see not one or two, but three, five, ten Carmens, all bad, I conclude that the rôle is difficult. Conversely, when I see the interpreters of Beckmesser being nearly always good, I conclude that Beckmesser is an easy rôle.

Carmen demands of an interpreter perhaps the hardest quality of all if it does not come naturally: audacity, of all the sentiments or feelings that a singer must discover. If one has not got it naturally, one is obliged to force, and one becomes a poor race-horse who is overstrained right to the end. I have often sung Carmen, and I know that everything is agitated. It must be sung and acted in a breathless manner all the time. It is not a question of the singer's powers of endurance, it is the rôle itself that is killing — orchestra, scenery, everything. I have asked many interpreters of the rôle and all are agreed in finding it a killing one — one simply never stops.

Let us now take the score. I have the impression that Carmen's entry could be understood and interpreted in several ways. There could be a number of Carmens quite different from each other, and all equally true.

One tragedy for singers is the absence of producers. None of our opera houses has a real producer, of that I am quite certain: I have worked enough with them to know. It is the reign of mediocrity and convention. We have seen many cases in recent years of interpreters who have been imperfect but full of character, spoilt by a producer who had concealed their natural talent by a stupid convention.

'Carmen, dis-nous quel jour tu nous aimeras. . . ?' A marvellously prepared entry. There are the cigarette-girls and the soldiers, but for me, in all current productions, Carmen is already too much in evidence in the front of the stage, with too many noisy gestures; whereas the situation subtly underlined by a real actress would be understood by everyone. After the aria 'Amour est un oiseau' when sung by such a Carmen — ardent, sensual (and how sensual!) — we come to a dialogue.

I take Mérimée's text: 'Each one paid her some compliments . . .' [Mme Croiza here read alternately the dialogue in Mérimée and that in the Meilhac and Halévy libretto]. In the mind of the librettists there is an uproar here that surrounds their character, while on the stage, the character is left too isolated. Everyone draws aside, makes a space round her. She forms the centre.

Convention and tradition are always confused. The whole rôle of Carmen is given in a stupid convention with which tradition has nothing to do. Carmen is a savage, who steals, who does not hesitate to slash a comrade's face with a knife. No operatic Carmen has enough real wildness for that.

Micaela and Escamillo are invented characters. I always have the impression, when they enter, of people who have got out of a lift at the wrong floor.

Convention has even acted against the music, against Bizet's wonderful stage-music. It has become a habit to make unbelievable pauses and to introduce play-acting [jeux de scènes], so that the singer is told by the producer:

'Madame, here you make the dagger thrust?'

'No, I don't make the dagger thrust.'

'Then here you make the gesture with the cigarette?'

'No . . . what is this gesture with the cigarette?'

and then he explains to you some piece of stage business which has become an established habit and that has no real connection with anything.

I think that the greatest actor is the one who creates a character in the simplest possible manner. But in our opera houses it is the exact opposite. 'Je pense à certain officier . . .', one could sing this simply, instead of complicating it. Our Carmens move all the time, but immobility forms part of her attraction. 'Je ne pars pas . . . je suis amoureuse . . .', this too is underlined too much. In all rôles, there are words of different importance and if all the words are underlined it is tantamount to cancelling everything.

In the scene of Jose's intended departure and Carmen's indignation, again too much is made of it immediately, which prevents a rise of dramatic intensity later.

Then comes the so-called 'Flower Song' which is so ardent, so tragic. It is after this 'Romance' that Carmen feels, with her marvellous feminine instinct, that she must take José more seriously: and there Bizet has put in a number of perfect musical nuances that are usually not even looked at.

One day at the Opéra-Comique, by chance, I heard this passage rehearsed by Garden. Even when she made a mistake (or at least when I thought she made a mistake), she had an essentially dramatic and living quality. 'Qui va là? Qui va là? . . . tais . . . toi . . . tais . . . toi. . . .' Usually this 'tais . . . toi. . . .' is shouted but Garden did it with nothing. Once again she pointed to the truth. Garden was certainly not Spanish, but this excellent actress restored to the rôle its balance of opéra-comique, that is to say, of comedy, of life.

The end is admirably simple and well-paced in Bizet: the dialogue with Jose and her death, of which I have spoken — I know of nothing more moving, more dramatic.

It is impossible to enumerate the things distorted by producers in this last act. The libretto does not follow Mérimée of course, but again there is no need to add grandiloquence and to distort life. I have a delightful memory of the Japanese theatre that came to Paris a few years ago. I did not understand any of the words, but, by the sole raising of the tone, the delivery, everything culminated in a paroxysm and in death, without a single gesture. Our operatic art is ruined by gestures, by undisciplined running about on the stage, by useless agitation. My last word of advice to interpreters is that it is not Mérimée's Carmen that we have to interpret, it is the one by Meilhac and Halévy and Bizet. We must remain with these three then; but if we want to add an element of simplicity to our whole interpretation, we can go back to Mérimée for inspiration.

3. PELLÉAS ET MÉLISANDE BY DEBUSSY

A propos of *Pelléas*, I will begin by reading a letter from Debussy which appeared in the *Monde musical* under the title, 'Why I wrote *Pelléas*':

> After several years of ardent pilgrimage to Bayreuth, I began to have doubts about the Wagnerian formula, or rather it seemed to me it could only serve the particular case of Wagner's genius. He was a great collector of formulas; he reassembled them in a form that appeared personal. . . , and, without denying his genius, one can say that he had put the final touch to the music of his day, rather as Victor Hugo swallowed up all the poetry (of his day) before him — therefore, one had to search for something later than Wagner, not 'after Wagner'.
> The drama of *Pelléas* which, in spite of its atmosphere of a dream, contains much more humanity and youth than the so-called documentaries on life, seemed to me admirably suited to what I wished to do. There is in it an evocative language whose feeling could find its prolongation in music and the orchestral scenery — I have tried to obey a law of beauty that seems to be singularly forgotten when it is a question of dramatic music. The characters of this drama try to sing like natural people, and not in an arbitrary language made up of traditions. It is from this that comes

the reproach that has been made against my so-called *parti pris* of monotonous declamation, where nothing, or no melody, ever appears. First of all, that is untrue. Furthermore, the feelings of a character cannot express themselves continually in a melodious fashion; then again, dramatic melody should be quite other than melody in general. The people who go to listen to music in the theatre, resemble those that one sees gathered round street singers. There, for two sous, one can procure melodic emotions for oneself. One can also state that among many subscribers to the state subsidized theatres, a will to understand is totally absent.

[Mme Croiza then said:] One of the most important points that I want to make to those who wish to interpret *Pelléas*, and to a conductor anxious to get a performance that is, I will not say magnificently sensitive, but exact (which is not the same thing), is that for *Pelléas* there is a necessary *youthfulness*. If *Pelléas* remains in too sombre an atmosphere, too 'old château', in spite of all the admiration that we may have for this *chef-d'oeuvre*, the performance becomes boring. There is in *Pelléas* a section that I will call 'the exit from the grotto'. 'Ah!' cries Pelléas, 'at last I can breathe — I thought I was going to faint in those huge caverns.'

This aspect of young love is so deep and yet so naïve between Pelléas and Mélisande, who is wilting in this old castle, and who is suffocating because in her there is youth and the need to live. One cannot say the exact ages of Pelléas and Mélisande, but they are two children lost in this dark château, and that which draws them together immediately, that which provokes this marvellous contact, full of sparks, is their youth.

Pelléas is pure, full of enthusiasm, and full of love, when he sees this beautiful Mélisande. For Mélisande is beautiful; we find the description of her in Maeterlinck's work stressed much more than in that of Debussy. It is this beauty that struck Golaud and that he describes in the letter read by Geneviève.

I also advise Geneviève not to be too solemn. She should not be the same age as Arkel! I will quote in this context the reflection of a witty spectator who, at the Opéra-Comique during the reading of this letter, said, 'My goodness, it is a letter from Proust!', because it seemed endless. Let us beware: Geneviève is much younger than Arkel and we must be able to feel this difference in age. I advise the Genevièves who will read the Letter, to read it at the tempo of declamation: 'Voici ce qu'il écrit à son frère Pelléas . . .'. It must be read simply, with a great gentleness and without sadness, because Geneviève wants to convince the old man, and to be able to say at the end: 'Be sure to light the lamp from this evening onwards, Pelléas . . .' (signifying Arkel's permission for Golaud to return home with Mélisande).

I remember having taken part in a performance in which everyone was sad. Pelléas was sad and uneasy and Mélisande was sad. Therefore, when I said to Pelléas: 'Be sure to light the lamp . . .' I said within myself to the audience: 'My good friends, there is the last smile you will get from now until the end of the performance — Salute it! It is the only one.' For again at once everyone became important, grave and old.

Let one read this letter at the speed of speech — it is a recitative, and in a recitative one must never slow up without a reason — compare the way Bruno Walter made his singers perform their recitatives in *Don Giovanni* — so alive and so rapid. Do not let us make Geneviève sad, do not make every sound a fatality, do not let us forget that her one aim is to obtain Golaud's return.

There are incidentally, passages in Golaud's letter (in Maeterlinck) that have not been set to music, such as the following: 'At the very moment that I found her by the stream, a golden crown had slipped from her hair and fallen into the water; moreover she was dressed like a princess, although her clothes had been torn by the briars. It is now six months since I married her and I know no more of her than on the day of our first meeting etc . . .'. And he ended by saying: 'But I am frightened of Arkel, in spite of all his kindness', to which Arkel replies: 'I say nothing about it; he has done what he had to do'.

Arkel must remain the doyen of the performance, the others must not join him: old age is not contagious. And Arkel goes on to say: 'How can you want me to judge what others have done? He [Golaud] has passed the age of maturity and if he marries, like a child, a little girl that he finds near a stream, it seems strange to us because we only see the reverse side of our destinies. Since the death of his wife, he lived only for his son, the little Yniold, and if he were going to marry, it would be because you wanted him to do so . . .' (Golaud was supposed to marry a Princess Ursula).

Here, I want to point out that we never sing Debussy's music 'exactly' enough. I want to warn those who put in accents where Debussy has not marked any. It is sometimes very difficult to avoid these accents. Let us be careful of this 'petit Yniold', it is always on the first beat of the bar — and eventually becomes exasperating.

Everyone knows the fervent admiration I have always had for Mary Garden, and one cannot speak of *Pelléas* without pronouncing her name. Here is what Debussy said of her in an article that appeared in *Musica* in 1908:

In the year 1902, when the Opéra-Comique put on *Pelléas* with such well-known care, I experienced these impressions: the character of Mélisande had always appeared to me difficult of realization. I tried hard to give it musically the fragility and distant charm; there remained her attitude, her long silences that a gesture could betray, or even render incomprehensible. And above all Mélisande's voice, heard inwardly, so tender; what was it going to be when the most beautiful voice in the world can become the unconscious enemy of the expression fitting a particular character?

It is not my affair, any more than to my taste, to speak here about the diverse phases through which one passes during the work of rehearsals. These were, however, the best among my hours in the theatre. I experienced inestimable moments and some very great artists. Among the latter appeared a curiously individual artist; there was hardly ever anything to say to her and little by little she assumed the character of Mélisande. I waited with a singular confidence mixed with curiosity. At last came the fifth act, the death of Mélisande, and I was so astonished I cannot express my emotion: it was the soft voice I had heard inwardly, with the faltering tenderness, and an art so moving that I had not believed it possible until then; and since when the public has bowed in admiration, with an ever growing fervour, before the name of Mary Garden.

I think that nearly all the listeners who are here have heard Mary Garden. I think that she will never be surpassed. I do not say that she will never be equalled, that would be too sad, and we do not know; but until now, no one has given like her this 'strange aspect', young and profound, of the rôle of Mélisande.

Now, I would like to tell you some of the appreciations that have been written of *Pelléas*. I do not choose them in order to show you the opinions that the first *performance* of *Pelléas* evoked, but for *Pelléas* itself, and not for the opinions of others. However, we are talking about a work which is only thirty years old — a mere nothing in the lifetime of an opera — and the growing success of *Pelléas* justifies the views of certain people who saw clearly, from the first, perhaps because they were already initiated. Many of them knew Debussy and realized that, even if they did not completely appreciate the inexpressible charm of his music, they were in the presence of a born musician, a creator, a true musical genius. I think that errors would be fewer if, more often, we knew the creators. Everyone in our domain (I do not dare say especially we women, it would sound too pretentious), when we approach artists and creators, if we have a little intelligence or feeling, even when we do not agree with their immediate manner of expression, know very well how to recognize that we are before 'someone'. We have this experience very often with painters, sculptors, musicians, and with their works! We feel that the first contact surpasses our intelligence and our possibilities, but we sense at once that we are before a work, before a *being*. This work, and this being, do not speak to us directly, completely, because they are beyond us. We are not ripe, we are not sufficiently advanced to seize them in their totality, but we are consciously troubled, and feel very small.

I think that for *Pelléas* it is so, too. Many musicians who had the good fortune to know Debussy, who followed him, were in permanent contact with his intelligence, his sensitive feeling, his musicality, his originality. (And one may well say originality, as it is related to a new work, a new way of expression, above all in the theatre — if indeed there be anything new under the sun, for, if we make a curve, we rediscover relationships with very ancient composers and musicians.) Those then who heard *Pelléas*, even if at their first performance they found this kind of continual recitative a little gloomy, even if they did not feel, from the first contact, the power, the originality, and the marvellous language of the composer, realized that they were in the presence of a great work. Many said to themselves, 'I have not understood it all, but I will come back; there is something new here, I must know it better to feel it more. I must accustom or "tame" myself, if one may put it that way.'

Questioned one day about the essence of the musical genius of his country, Claude Debussy replied, 'The musical genius of France is something like imagination, fantasy, within feeling or sensibility.' I found this in the preface to a volume of correspondence between Toulet and Debussy, and it is a definition that has always impressed me.

For me, as an interpreter, in this fusion of imagination, fantasy and sensibility of feeling, Debussy has described that which touches me closely in the art of self-expression of both creator and interpreter. All of us, here, know that we find sensibility or feeling in an interpreter much more often than one expects, but that imagination and fantasy is most often lacking. An interpreter is too frequently the same person, either a solemn person, or a gay one; but the character who changes his mentality, as in the theatre one changes one's costume, changing and bringing to the scene the suitable facial expression, remains extremely rare. I am more and more convinced of this. I am struck every day by real talents that for me lack variety. In spite of voice and feeling, they lack the kind of spice which sharpens curiosity by degrees, in the interpretation of a work, and which is due to change of physiognomy, to a change of intonation, to a kind of interior pirouette, one could say, which creates, for the listener and for the spectator, a variety, which, in my opinion, is absolutely indispensable.

I would like to read you some lines from *Debussy* by André Suarès:

> The greatness of *Pelléas* is hidden beneath the exact proportions and sobriety, and even the power. Never has anyone tried less after effect, never has anyone put so much reserve in being so tragic. Such discretion gives to tragedy an irresistible charm of modesty. All other music seems emphatic after this; there is something of antiquity, and of Racine in the scene of little Yniold with his father, and in that of Act IV between Golaud and Mélisande. Here, the expression is at once the most penetrating and the most savagely jealous. The fury of the accesses of frenzy, of the double cruelty of a jealous man to himself and towards his victim, create an atmosphere charged with suspicion and the convictions of uncertainty; one must recall *Roxane* and *Othello* to find anything to equal them. So much vigour in passion does not harm the delicacy of the feeling; the love scenes and the end have a gentle and profound melancholy, and an inimitable 'accent'. There are adorable phrases, akin to confidences, or the trace of tears on crystal; astonishing music that seems like the emotion of an idea within the transparent sheath of the word, phrases adorable because they are so right, and yet so general that their inflection appears to be the natural voice of the sentiment. The sensibility of the ardent Debussy is, above all, artistic and full of love.

I like this definition. . . . Further on we find, 'An unforgettable atmosphere envelops *Pelléas*. This music is a "climate" of feeling. Debussy gives the poem the real life it has not got, it makes men and women from marionettes, and fate from mere string. The dramas of Maeterlinck call for music. The wonderful unity of this music in *Pelléas* is an effect of balance, perhaps unique, between sensation and intelligence. . . . Debussy expresses by allusion that which others do not equally succeed in defining by multiplying the musical signs.'

In spite of such homage we are continually told that *Pelléas* has not been understood; it is true, it has not been understood by everyone, but what great work of art is, at its first impact, able to arouse enthusiasm amongst the general public? I think that all the great works of art begin by arousing astonishment. Then understanding comes, rather slowly, following the degree of culture and perception of the individual. A true work of art always ends in triumph.

EPILOGUE
by Betty Bannerman

In retrospect, the lessons and classes with Claire Croiza were like a wonderful voyage of discovery; a widening of interests accompanied by jewels of detail. She was never discouraging, but rarely wholly satisfied, so incentive was never lacking. She was critical of some of the feminine traits of that time, disliking gush, maudlin self-pity, and the leaning to sentimentality in the place of melancholy. Even in melancholy songs there is room for a smile of happy memories, she said. But her radiant smile when a 'victory' was gained, was reward indeed!

Of course there are elements a book cannot include, of the personal help and happiness I received from her friendship, and being welcomed into her family life at Bréthencourt in the countryside she loved. Here she could have calm and peace for short intervals in the ceaseless activity of Paris and her travels. Her faith and her belief in the 'good', whatever trials may befall, were accompanied by a generosity and kindness that were never denied to anyone in need.

She gave me the confidence I lacked, and she passed on the joy she found in so many things besides music and art. She was a wonderful comrade, sharing and enjoying humble amusements and interests.

*   *   *

Eighteen years have passed since I gave a talk, 'Recollections of Claire Croiza', to the British Institute of Recorded Sound, at Patrick Saul's invitation. This was at the time of the publication at my behest of EMI's two-sided LP record comprising some of Croiza's 78 recordings. Then, in 1984 Jean-Michel Nectoux set up the splendid exhibition, 'Hommage à Claire Croiza', at the Bibliothèque Nationale in Paris, aided by her son, Jean-Claude Honegger. Her name is therefore still with us.

I am well aware that, in this book, these translations of some of Croiza's Classes are inadequate to express what she gave to those who heard her. One cannot bring a vital personality to life in cold print. But I have become increasingly aware of the help Croiza's interpretations and advice are still able to give to singers and teachers. My great wish has been to be able to pass on to the young singers of this generation, who are so open to 'universal' ideas, something of what she gave me fifty years ago. Many of the singers and teachers who followed her, and were influenced by her classes, have incorporated her beliefs into their 'credos'. As a pebble thrown into a pond causes ever-widening circles, I hope this book may reach yet more singers and listeners and teachers.

B.B.

NOTES

BY PATRICK SAUL

ABRAHAM, Hélène   French amateur singer; married to the actor and writer Pierre Abraham; related by marriage to the poet Jean-Richard Bloch; first heard Croiza in 1913 in Paris in Monteverdi's *Il Coronazione di Poppea*; attended her courses at the École Normale de Musique 1930; from then until 1939 assisted in their organization and made shorthand notes (approved by Croiza) which formed the basis of her book *Un Art de l'interprétation Claire Croiza — Les cahiers d'un auditrice* (Paris: Office de Centralisation des Ouvrages, 1954).

ALAIN, Jehan Ariste (1911–1940)   French composer and organist; pupil of Marcel Dupré; killed during second world war.

APOLLINAIRE, Guillaume (pseud. of Wilhelm de Kostrowitzky) (1880–1918)   French poet of part Polish extraction, natural son of Angelica Kostrowitzky; born in Italy but educated in France; originally a Symbolist but under influence of Cubism and other modernist movements he made experiments such as his *Calligrammes* (word-pictures) and became a leader of the avant-garde; his influence on poets of his own and later generations was immense.

ARGENTINA, La (pseud. of Antonia Mercé) (1890–1936)   Spanish dancer, the most celebrated of her period; child of Spanish classical dancers; she devoted herself entirely to Spanish dance; apart from her subtle use of the castanets she was admired by Croiza as an artist who 'makes a profession of suppleness and rhythm; about whom there is no sense of haste; who takes her time when she enters or leaves the stage, and when she makes every gesture and executes every figure in her dance'.

BARDAC, Emma (née Moÿse) (1862–1934)   French amateur singer of professional standard; born into wealthy family; married, first, Sigismond Bardac (financier); her son Raoul was a pupil of Debussy; her daughter Hélène (Dolly) (later Mme Gaston de Tinan) was dedicatee of Fauré's *Dolly Suite* (1893–96); to Emma Bardac herself he dedicated *La Bonne chanson*. She married, second, Debussy, who dedicated the second set of *Fêtes galantes*, *Trois Chansons de France* and *Le Promenoir des deux amants* to her; to their daughter Claude-Emma (Chouchou) (1905–1919) Debussy dedicated *The Children's Corner*.

BASTIEN, Alfred-Théodore-Joseph (1873–1955) Belgian figurative painter of portraits and landscapes; studied at Académie Royale, Brussels and later professor there.

BAUDELAIRE, Charles Pierre (1821–67) French poet and critic; addicted to opium, and impoverished by extravagant tastes, at an early age he contracted the venereal disease which eventually killed him; he had a succession of political enthusiasms, left, right and centre, and lasting admiration for Delacroix and Wagner; despite the emotional disorder of his relatively short life, he found the time to write art criticism of the highest quality, an outstanding translation of the prose works of Poe — for whom he had feelings of spiritual kinship — and poetry, at once sensual and spiritual, which established him amongst the greatest French poets. Though a member of no school and the founder of none, his influence on the intellectual perceptions of succeeding generations has been immense.

BECKMESSER, Sixtus Baritone rôle in *Die Meistersinger*; a musically incompetent pedant and an object of scorn.

BELLAY, Joachim du (1522–60) French poet; born into noble family; originally inspired by Petrarch, he was later under the influence of Ronsard, with whom and others he collaborated in forming the *Pléiade* group (*qv*) for the reform of French poetry.

BERNARD, Anthony (1891–1963) British conductor.

BILITIS An imaginary poetess of Greek antiquity. The poems set by Debussy in his *Chansons de Bilitis* were really by Pierre Louÿs (*qv*).

BONNIER, Pierre (1861–1918) French doctor; laryngologist at Paris Clinique médicale de l'Hôtel-Dieu; controversial belief that nasal problems were at root of many illnesses; in lectures at the Paris Conservatoire (reported in a book published in 1907) he discussed physiological factors in different kinds of voices and rôles, citing changes in voice from baritone and bass to tenor (see under LHÉRIE, MARIO, MONGINI and RESZKE).

BONNIÈRES, Robert de (1850–1905) French poet and man of letters; member of Société Nationale de Musique (*qv*); friend of Duparc, who set his 'Le Manoir de Rosemonde'; lifelong friend and collaborator of d'Indy, for whom he provided song texts and opera libretti.

BOURGET, Paul Charles Joseph (1852–1935) French novelist and critic; Catholic; on political right.

BRÉVILLE, Pierre Onfroy de (1861–1949) French composer, teacher and critic; pupil of Dubois; also of Franck, with whom and the Schola Cantorum he was closely associated; wrote songs, instrumental, choral and orchestral works; Croiza created title rôle in Bréville's opera *Eros Vainqueur*, on 7 March 1910 at the Théâtre de la Monnaie in Brussels, at the composer's request.

BUSSINE, Romain (1830–99) French singing teacher at Paris Conservatoire; adapted anonymous Italian songs which were set by Fauré in the 'Sérénade toscane' and 'Après un rêve'; Fauré dedicated his song 'L'Absent' (a setting of a poem by Victor Hugo) to Bussine; with Saint-Saëns he founded the Société Nationale (*qv*) in 1871.

CAECILIA, La Chorale see under VOCHT.

CALZABIGI, Raniero di (1714–95) Italian poetaster, man of letters, librettist and financial practitioner; described by Casanova as 'worldly, astute, and fond of women'; his aesthetic ideal was to ally poetry not to music but to declamation; he followed Durazzo in seeking to purify opera and ballet by displacing the insipid libretti of Metastasio; he wrote the libretti of *Orfeo ed Euridice*, *Alceste* and *Paride ed Elena* for Gluck (*qv*).

CAPLET, André (1878–1925) French composer, conductor and pianist; pupil of Fauré, Woollett, Leroux, Vidal and Lenepveu; assistant conductor of Colonne Orchestra under Edouard Colonne; conductor of Théâtre de l'Odéon orchestra and (1910–14) of the Boston Symphony Orchestra; his works were much influenced by Debussy and Fauré; he worked closely with Debussy and conducted the first performance of *Le Martyre de Saint-Sébastien* in May 1911.

CARON, Rose (1857–1930) French dramatic soprano; studied at Paris Conservatoire where she was later a professor; début Brussels 1884; at Paris Opéra from 1885 where she gave first French performance of Elsa in *Lohengrin* in 1891.

CARVALHO, Caroline (née Félix-Miolan) (1827–95) Leading French operatic soprano of her day; début in *Lucia* and *La Juive* 1849; sang in the premières of Gounod's *Faust*, *Philémon et Baucis*, *Mireille* and *Roméo et Juliette*.

CHALUPT, René (1885–1957) French poet and writer; as a young man worked in piano store; wrote books about Gershwin and Ravel; his poems, in the style of Toulet (*qv*), were set by Roussel, Schmitt and Milhaud.

CHARLES D'ORLÉANS (1394–1465) French poet of courtly love; nephew of Charles VI and father of Louis XII; captured at Agincourt and a prisoner in England for 25 years.

CHEVALIER, Maurice (1888–1972) French music-hall singer, dancer, actor and author; partner of Mistinguett, Gaby Deslys and others; his career lasted for more than 60 years.

CHEVILLARD, Camille (1859–1923) French conductor and composer; son-in-law of Charles Lamoureux whom he followed as conductor of the Lamoureux Orchestra; refused to audition Croiza as a student; conducted first performance in France of Elgar's *Dream of Gerontius* with Croiza as the Angel — her first Paris concert — in 1906.

CLAUDEL, Paul-Louis-Charles-Marie (1868–1955) French mystic poet and dramatist; served in diplomatic service for 40 years; a devout Catholic; profoundly influenced in 1884 by reading Rimbaud; his plays are influenced by Greek drama.

COLETTE (1873–1954) French novelist; she wrote the libretto for Ravel's opera *L'Enfant et les sortilèges*.

COMMEDIA DELL'ARTE Popular comedy using stock characters such as Columbine and Harlequin; mainly improvised (as distinct from *Commedia erudità*, which was written down); frequently performed by groups of strolling players; originated in the 16th century in Italy, but widely influential outside its country of origin.

COOPER, Gerald (1892–1947) British writer on musical subjects and, from 1922, promoter of concerts of early and contemporary music.

COPEAU, Jacques (1879–1949) French theatre director, producer, actor and writer; associated with Gide in foundation of the *Nouvelle Revue Française* (1908); he founded in 1913 the *Théâtre du Vieux-Colombier* in the Paris street of that name; this was a literary theatre, linked to the *NRF*; Copeau's object was to purify the French theatre by replacing what was conventional — star-studded, sentimental or crudely realistic — with productions based on truth, unpretentious decor and a respect for the actor and for the French language. Copeau left the Vieux-Colombier in 1924 and formed the nucleus of the *Compagnie des Quinze*.

COPPÉE, François (1842–1908) French playwright, poet and critic; he wrote about youthful love and the lives of the poor.

CORTOT, Alfred (1877–1962) French pianist, conductor, lecturer, teacher, editor and writer on music; pupil of Louis Diémer; répétiteur at Bayreuth 1896; founded the famous trio, with

Thibaud and Casals, in 1905, and the École Normale de Musique in 1920; exponent of Chopin, Schumann and the German classics; also of French composers of the 20th century, many of whose works he created; the greatest French pianist and one of the most remarkable musical minds of the century; accompanied Croiza on various occasions.

COURTNEIDGE, Cicely (1893–1980)   British comedienne married to Jack Hulbert.

CRAIG, Gordon (1872–1966)   English actor, scenic designer and writer on the theatre; son of Ellen Terry; in his widely influential writings he advocated artistic unity, achieved by overall control of a play by a single producer; he was against realism and proposed the use of movable scenery and changing lighting which, rather than imitating reality, would be purely suggestive.

CROS, Charles (1842–88)   French poet, author of humorous monologues, and inventor; he wrote a paper describing a theoretical method of recording sound on 18 April 1877; Edison constructed his own similar invention during the same year.

CURIE, Marie (1867–1934)   French physicist, born in Poland; wife of Pierre Curie (1859–1906), with whom she investigated the properties of radium and radio-activity.

DEBUSSY, Claude (1862–1918)   French composer, pianist and critic; Debussy first accompanied Croiza in 1913 in some of his songs when, at short notice, she replaced Rose Féart; he also accompanied her at concerts in aid of war charities during March 1917.

DELACROIX, Eugène (1798–1863)   French painter; a leader of the Romantic movement; opposed to the classicism represented by Ingres.

DEPAGE, Antoine (1862–1925)   Belgian surgeon; professor at University of Brussels from 1907; leading part in organizing medical services during first world war.

DESTOUCHES, André-Cardinal (1672–1749)   French composer of songs and operas; superintendent of the King's music and for a time director of the Opéra.

DOMMANGE, René (1888–1977)   French poet, music publisher and authority on copyright law.

DOYEN, Jean (1907–19?)   French pianist; pupil of Marguerite Long, whom he succeeded as professor at the Paris Conservatoire; remarkable for the range of his repertoire and for interpretative as well as technical ability; took part in many of Croiza's *causeries* as accompanist and soloist; played relatively little outside France.

DUBAS, Marie (1894–1972) French music-hall singer; début at 14; original career in operetta; at the Olympia music-hall in Paris in 1927 her singing of the song 'Pedro', described as a 'fantaisie hispano-montmartroise' made her famous. Following the example of her idol, Yvette Guilbert, she included in her programmes folk songs, comic songs and songs of realism and tragedy. Of Marie Dubas, Edith Piaf said, 'she was my model, the example I wanted to follow'.

DUPARC, Henri (Marie Eugène Henri Fouques-Duparc) (1848–1933) French composer; pupil of Franck; one of the founders of the Société Nationale; from 1885 he suffered from a psychological disorder which prevented him from composing for the rest of his life; he destroyed most of his earliest works though a few for orchestra and for piano were published; his fame rests on 16 songs which, though showing the influence of Franck and Wagner, are among the most original and profound songs of the 19th century. He much admired Croiza's singing, as the two letters dated 17 October 1914 and 14 April 1916 show. They are given as an appendix on pp. 187–9.

DUSE, Eleanore (1859–1924) Italian actress; born into a family of actors, she appeared on the stage at the age of four; a woman of great culture and a wide range of intellectual interests; a close friend of Boito (the composer and Verdi's librettist), and of D'Annunzio, who wrote plays for her; she had great international success in works across a wide spectrum; she was celebrated for the beauty of her voice and for the subtlety, and sometimes the volcanic passion, of her performances.

ELISABETH, Queen of Belgium (1876–1965) daughter of Duke Charles Theodore of Bavaria; wife of Albert I, King of the Belgians from 1909; violin pupil of Ysaÿe; established various charities and prizes in aid of composers and musical performers.

FAURÉ, Gabriel Urbain (1845–1924) French composer, organist, pianist and teacher. Croiza was introduced to Fauré by Gounod's widow; he was so taken with her singing of 'Les Berceaux' that he asked her to repeat it several times; at the end of her performance in *Pénélope* he said, 'how happy I am to have for once heard my music performed as I wrote it'; Croiza, accompanied by Fauré, gave the first performance of *Le Jardin clos* on 28 January 1915; he dedicated 'Dans la nymphée', a song in the set, to her; accompanied by Cortot (*qv*) she took part in a concert in honour of Fauré given at the Sorbonne on 20 June 1922, in the presence of the composer and the President of the Republic; she sang *La Bonne chanson*, in the version with strings and piano, directed by Cortot, at the École Normale de Musique on 23 June 1935.

FISHER, Esther (Esther Lady Barran) (b. 1901)   British pianist; born in New Zealand; pupil in Paris of Isidore Philipp and Philip Emmanuel; greatly influenced in her youth by Busoni; Professor at Royal College of Music, London.

FORT, Paul (1872–1960)   French poet; influenced by Gide and Verlaine; with Valéry edited the journal *Vers et prose* (1905–14); founded an avant-garde theatre; works include historical dramas and *Ballades françaises*, folkloric in style.

FRANÇOIS DE SALES, Saint (1567–1622)   French Catholic moralist; Bishop of Geneva from 1602; his sermons and writings, rational rather than mystic, couched in simple terms, exerted great influence in all classes of society.

FUGÈRE, Lucien (1848–1935)   French baritone; début 1870 Ba-Ta-Clan café-concerts; at Bouffes-Parisiens in operetta from 1874; at Opéra-Comique from 1877; created about 40 rôles in works by Chabrier, Massenet, Messager, Saint-Saëns and others; his was one of the most remarkable careers in French operatic history, for he was still singing at 85.

GARCIA, Manuel Patricio Rodriguez (1805–1906)   Spanish singer and singing teacher, the first to make a scientific study of voice production; from 1848 at Royal Academy of Music in London; pupils included Jenny Lind, Mathilde Marchesi, Julius Stockhausen and Sir Charles Santley; brother of Pauline Viardot (*qv*).

GARDEN, Mary (1874–1967)   Scottish soprano; educated in the United States; pupil in Paris of Marchesi, Trabadello and Fugère; début 1900 Opéra-Comique in *Louise*; created many rôles there including Mélisande in *Pelléas et Mélisande* in 1902; retired from the stage 1931.

GAUTHIER-VILLARS, Henry (1859–1931)   French poet, playwright, novelist and musical and literary critic who often wrote as 'Willy'; one time husband of Colette; Wagnerian, and early supporter of Debussy.

GAUTIER, Théophile (1811–72)   French poet, novelist, critic and essayist; a leader of the Romantic movement.

GHÉON, Henri (pseud. of Henri Vangeon) (1875–1944)   French poet and author of religious and other plays and of biographies.

GIESEKING, Walter (1895–1956)   German pianist; born in Lyons of German parents. Having a photographic memory he could memorize a complex score away from the piano; repertoire embraced almost the entire piano literature; especially admired for his interpretation of Ravel and Debussy.

GILES, Herbert Allen (1845–1935)   British civil servant, scholar and writer; in consular service in China for many years; professor of Chinese at Cambridge University 1897–1932; translated 8/9th century Chinese poets (see Roché).

GLUCK, Christoph Willibald von (1714–87)   German composer, first of Italian, then of French operas; until 1754 most of the operas he encountered were Italian, often with libretti by Metastasio, but in that year he was engaged as Kapellmeister by Count Giacomo Durazzo, intendant of the Viennese theatres, a cultured man and the prime mover in the regeneration of the *opera seria*. It was the ideas of Durazzo which in due course led to the collaboration between Gluck and Calzabigi (*qv*) and thus to Gluck's reforms: dethronement of the virtuoso singer; fusion of recitative and aria within a musical entity; rejection of conventional historical subjects in favour of what was genuinely human.

GOURMONT, Rémy de (1858–1915)   French poet, critic and polymath; influenced by Mallarmé and Huysmans and in turn a great influence on the next generation of French writers through his articles in the journal *Mercure de France* of which he was a founder and co-editor.

GRANDMOUGIN, Charles Jean (1850–1930)   French poet and writer on aesthetics, and on Wagner and other musical subjects; his poetry, often based on devotion to his native Franche-Comté, was set by Fauré (*Poème d'un jour*), Godard, Pugno, Thomé and others; he wrote libretto for Franck's opera *Hulda*.

GROVLEZ, Gabriel (1879–1944)   French composer and conductor; pupil of Diémer, Gédalge and Fauré; influenced by Charles Bordes; professor at Schola Cantorum and Paris Conservatoire; chorus master at Opéra-Comique 1911–13; conducted premières of the orchestral version of Fauré's *Dolly Suite* and of Roussel's *Le Festin de l'araignée*.

GUILBERT, Yvette (1867–1944)   French diseuse; as a girl was mannequin, shop-assistant and dressmaker; from 1885 she had walk-on parts in Paris theatres where, she said, she received 'wonderful free lessons from the leading actors of the day' which taught her how to move, speak and relate to an audience; in 1889 she made her début at the Eldorado music-hall; a completely original and individual artist, her repertoire contrasted contemporary satirical songs by Xanrof and Bruant with songs from the Renaissance; she was painted, in her yellow dress and long black gloves, many times by Toulouse-Lautrec.

GUITRY, Lucien (1860–1925)   French actor; encouraged as a young man by Bernhardt, with whom he appeared on the stage; admired for the restraint and lack of gestures, without which he could yet express convincingly emotions of great subtlety or violent passion; he acted in a wide variety of plays including some by his son Sacha (*qv*).

GUITRY, Sacha (1885–1957)   French actor, prolific playwright, theatre and film director; son of Lucien Guitry; married four times, his first wife being Yvonne Printemps.

HAHN, Reynaldo (1875–1947)   French composer, baritone, pianist, conductor and writer on singing and other musical subjects; pupil of Dubois, Lavignac and Massenet; close friend of Proust; conducted *Don Giovanni* at Salzburg Festival, 1906; director Paris Opéra 1947; as baritone he often accompanied himself; wrote piano, chamber and orchestral works, ballets, incidental music, operettas and operas; also songs, some of the most popular having been written in his early teens.

HALÉVY, Jacques-François-Fromental (pseud. of Elias Lévy) (1799–1862)   French composer; pupil of Cherubini at the Paris Conservatoire; teacher there of Bizet, Gounod, Lecocq etc; best known work is *La Juive*; with Meilhac wrote text of Bizet's *Carmen*.

HONEGGER, Arthur (1892–1955)   Swiss composer born in France. Teachers included the Swiss Friedrich Hégar and, in France, Widor, Gédalge and (for violin) Lucien Capet and (conducting) Vincent d'Indy. His musical sympathies were as much German as French; although linked by ties of friendship to Auric, Milhaud and Poulenc, fellow members of 'Les Six' (*qv*), he moved away from the ideals of his youth towards what he described as 'music in its most serious and austere aspects'.

HUGO, Victor Marie (1802–85)   French poet, dramatist, novelist and politician; the principal writer of the Romantic school in France in terms of both quantity and quality, though his output included much that was sentimental or grandiloquent; he is nevertheless considered by many to be the greatest of all French poets. During the third empire he lived in exile in Guernsey.

INDY, Vincent d' (1871–1931)   French composer, conductor, teacher, writer and editor; born into a musical family of the nobility; pupil of Marmontel and Diémer (piano), Lavignac and Franck (composition); he wrote a biography of Franck, in furtherance of whose ideas he, Charles Bordes and Guilmant founded in 1894 the Schola Cantorum, a teaching institution; he wrote songs, piano, chamber and orchestral works, and operas.

INGHELBRECHT, Désiré-Émile (1880–1965) French conductor, composer and writer; a close friend of Debussy; conducted première of Debussy's *Marche écossaise* (1913); wrote songs, chamber and orchestral works, ballets and an opera.

JANSEN, Jacques (b. 1913) French baritone; pupil of Jouvet, Panzèra and Croiza at Paris Conservatoire; first singing engagements were for the French radio; début Opéra-Comique 1941 in *Pelléas et Mélisande*, since when he has had an international career.

JEAN-AUBRY, Georges (1882–1949) French writer on music, and propagandist for contemporary French music; editor in London of the *Chesterian* journal from 1919, and organizer of concerts of French music; author of *La Musique française d'aujourd'hui* and *La Musique et les nations* etc.; translated novels by Conrad into French.

JOURDAN-MORHANGE, Hélène (1892–1961) French violinist; pupil of Nadaud, Enesco and Capet. She was one of Ravel's closest friends and wrote books entitled *Ravel et nous* and (with Vlado Perlemuter) *Ravel d'après Ravel*. Ravel dedicated his Violin Sonata to her. As the leader of a string quartet she collaborated from 1918 with Jane Bathori, Pierre Bertin and others in the concerts of 'Les Nouveaux Jeunes', the nucleus out of which grew 'Les Six' (*qv*).

JUYOL, Suzanne (b. 1920) French soprano; studied at Paris Conservatoire; début 1942 Opéra-Comique; at Opéra from 1945.

KAHN, Micheline (1889–19?) French harpist, pupil at Paris Conservatoire of Adolphe Hasselmans; gave first performance of Ravel's *Introduction et allegro* (1907) and of Fauré's *La Châtelaine en sa tour* (dedicated to her) (1918). Caplet wrote two *Divertissements* for her.

KLINGSOR, Tristan (1874–1966) (pseud. of Léon Leclerc) French Symbolist poet; also a painter, composer and writer on aesthetic subjects.

KREISLER, Fritz (1875–1962) Austrian violinist and composer; pupil of Hellmesberger and Bruckner in Vienna; of Massart (for violin) and Delibes (for composition) at Paris Conservatoire. One of the greatest violinists in musical history.

KUFFERATH, Maurice (1852–1919) Belgian conductor, cellist and pro-Wagnerian writer on music; originally studied law and the history of art; editor of *Le Guide musical*; director and chief conductor of the Théâtre de la Monnaie in Brussels 1900–14.

LAFORGUE, Jules (1860–87) French poet who died of consumption; his poetry, melancholy with an underlay of cynical humour, tended towards Symbolism and was widely influential.

LAHOR, Jean (pseud. of Henri Cazalis; also known as Jean Caselli) (1840–1909)   French pessimist Parnassian poet; doctor, and writer on medical subjects; moved in artistic circles in France (Maupassant, Saint-Saëns, Augusta Holmès and Mallarmé) and England (Ruskin, William Morris and Burne-Jones).

LALO, Charles (1877–1953)   French musical aesthetician.

LALO, Pierre (1866–1943)   French music critic of the *Journal des débats* and, 1898–1914, of *Le Temps*. He was hostile to admirers of Debussy; son of the composer Edouard Lalo.

LAMARTINE, Alphonse-Marie-Louis (1790–1869)   French royalist poet, diplomat and politician; the first important poet of the Romantic movement in France, much influenced by Chateaubriand; his poems, which deal with love and religion, though impulsive and highly individual, are mild and sentimental in tone.

LARA, Isidore de (1858–1935)   English composer, principally of operas, in the style of Massenet and Saint-Saëns; the best known are *The Light of Asia* and *Messalina*.

LECONTE DE LISLE, Charles-Marie-René (1818–94)   French poet; leader of the Parnassians (*qv*); and translator of the classics; essentially pessimist and atheist, Leconte de Lisle aims to depict nature and the lives of mankind and of animals at differing times and places.

LEHMANN, Lilli (1848–1929)   German soprano; daughter of opera singers; acted as accompanist to her mother from age of 12 and studied singing with her; début in minor rôle in *The Magic Flute* in 1865 but at next performance had to take over the rôle of Pamina; sang Helmwige and the First Rhinemaiden at the opening Bayreuth Festival in 1876 and performed at the Salzburg Mozart Festival in 1905. One of the greatest singers in both opera and the *Lied*.

LE ROY, Grégoire (1862–1941) Belgian poet, painter and designer.

LHÉRIE, Pierre (1844–1937)   French tenor; originally baritone; Don Jose in première of *Carmen* at Opéra-Comique 3 March 1865.

L'HERMITE, Tristan (1601–55) (pseud. of François L'Hermite) French playwright and poet; one of the founders of French classical drama.

LORRAIN, Jean (1855–1906)   French poet and satirical literary critic.

LOUŸS, Pierre (pseud. of Pierre-Félix Louis) (1870–1925)   French poet, moralist and classical scholar. A close friend, and virtual literary adviser, of Debussy; also associated with Leconte de Lisle, Hérédia and other Parnassians and with Valéry. He wrote the *Chansons de Bilitis*, first said to be by a Greek poetess.

LULLY, Jean Baptiste (originally Giambattista Lulli) (1632–87)

French composer born in Florence of Italian parentage; largely self-taught; entered service of Louis XIV in 1652 as dancer, violinist and composer; established opera in Paris; granted virtual royal monopoly in the production of opera throughout France; wrote music for Molière's ballet-comedies, orchestral and choral music and operas.

LUSH, Ernest (1908–88)   British pianist; pupil of Tobias Matthay and Carl Friedberg; BBC staff accompanist 1928–66.

MADELAINE, Stéphen de la (pseud. of Etienne Jean Baptiste Madelaine) singer, singing teacher and writer about the voice; soloist at the *Chapelle de la Musique Particulière* of Charles X (who reigned 1824–1830); author of *Théories complètes du chant* (Paris 1852), *Etudes pratiques de style* and *Physiologie du chant*; critical of contemporary singing teachers 'who are at peace with the world and with themselves while enjoying the fruits of their charlatanism'; believed that given suitable training even an average voice could conquer any difficulty.

MAETERLINCK, Maurice (1862–1945)   Belgian Symbolist poet and dramatist; his plays, which are philosophical, mystical and enigmatic, include *Ariane et Barbe-bleue* (on which Dukas based his opera), *Pelléas et Mélisande* (the inspiration for Debussy's opera and also for a work by Schoenberg) and *L'Oiseau bleu*.

MALLARMÉ, Stéphane (Étienne Mallarmé) (1842–98)   French poet, the principal Symbolist of his period; influenced by Baudelaire, Banville and, particularly, by Poe, whose poems he translated; for many years a teacher of English; weekly meetings of poets, painters and musicians in his apartment encouraged cross-fertilization between the arts. In Mallarmé's later poems concentration of thought leads to obscurity; the poet's aim was to express not reality itself but the essence behind it.

MANGEOT, André (1883–1970)   French violinist, long resident in England; organized chamber-music concerts; in 1919 established (and led) the International String Quartet; was director of ensemble music at the universities of Oxford and Cambridge.

MANGEOT, Auguste   French musicologist and critic; editor of *Le Monde Musical*; in 1919, with Cortot (*qv*), founded the École Normale de Musique.

MARGUERITE DE NAVARRE (1492–1549)   French poet and playwright; daughter of Charles d'Orléans (*qv*); sister of Francis I; her second husband was Charles, King of Navarre; she had political and literary interests and influence; her works are often religious in spirit.

MARIO, Giovanni Matteo (1810–83)   Italian tenor; originally army officer; début Paris Opéra 1838 in *Robert le Diable*; international reputation for elegant style and exceptional beauty of voice; second husband of Giulia Grisi (1811–69), who was admired by Bellini and Rossini; Donizetti wrote duo in *Don Pasquale* for Mario and Grisi (see under BONNIER).

MATON, Adolphe (1839–?)   Belgian teacher of singing, pianist and conductor; naturalized French 1872; studied at Brussels Conservatoire under Fétis (composition) and Michelet (piano); head of singing at Monnaie in Brussels; later taught singing in London and Paris; conductor of Mapleson's London company and at the Paris Opéra; he was Croiza's second voice teacher.

MAURANE, Camille (b. 1911)   French baritone; pupil of Croiza at Paris Conservatoire; also sang in his youth as Camille Moreau; début Opéra-Comique 1940.

MEILHAC, Henri (1831–97)   French playwright; see under Halévy.

MÉRIMÉE, Prosper (1803–70)   French novelist; a friend of Stendhal and Turgenev; translator of some of Pushkin's works; his novels and stories are mostly historical in subject matter and romantic in tone; the best known is *Carmen*, on which Bizet's opera is based.

MICHEAU, Janine (1914–76)   French soprano; pupil at the Toulouse and Paris Conservatoires; début Opéra-Comique as Cherubino, 1933; for many years principal soprano at the Paris Opéra.

MIKHAËL, Ephraïm (pseud. of Georges Ephraïm Michel) (1866–90)   French Symbolist poet; with Catulle Mendès librettist of Chabrier's unfinished *Briséis*.

MILHAUD, Darius (1892–1974)   French composer, pianist and conductor; born into wealthy Provençal family; pupil of Leroux, Gédalge, Widor, d'Indy and Dukas; much influenced by his stay during first world war in Brazil as secretary to Claudel (*qv*) (cf *Le Boeuf sur le toit* and *Saudades do Brasil*) and by hearing American jazz at the Hammersmith Palais de Danse in 1920 (cf *La Création du monde*); he wrote more than 400 works, in every medium; he played at at least one of Croiza's *causeries*.

MONGINI, Pietro (1830–74)   Italian tenor; until 1853 sang bass rôles in Italy; début Paris 1855 and praised for his vocal brilliance in tenor rôle of Edgardo in *Lucia di Lammermoor* (see under BONNIER).

MONNAIE, Théâtre de la   The most important Belgian opera house, situated on the site of a mint; founded in 1700.

MORAX, René (1873–1963)   Swiss poet, playwright and theatre director; associated with Swiss composer Gustave Doret in 1905 revival of *Fête des Vignerons* etc.; produced Honegger's biblical dramas *Judith* (text by Morax) and *Le Roi David*; involved in renaissance of popular theatre; with his painter brother Jean founded open-air *Théâtre du Jorat* at Mézières (Switzerland) 1908.

MORÉAS, Jean (pseud. of Iannis Papadiamantopoulos) (1856–1910) French poet of Greek parentage; originally Symbolist, later tending towards neo-classicism.

MOTTL, Felix (1856–1911) Austrian conductor; pupil of Hellmesberger, Door and Bruckner; assistant to Wagner at Bayreuth; chief conductor there in 1886; edited and conducted works by Berlioz.

MUSSET, Alfred Louis Charles de (1810–57) French Romantic poet, playwright and novelist; a liaison with Georges Sand in 1833 led to a rupture which affected Musset very deeply; his plays, a few of which are in verse, mingle the terrible, the absurd and the comic; they are sometimes satirical and there is usually a tragic underlay.

NARÇON, Armand (1875–19?) French bass; member of Paris Opéra company for 30 years from 1902; in leading rôles from 1911; professor at Paris Conservatoire from 1934.

OLÉNINE D'ALHEIM, Marie (1869–1970) French singer famous from 1896 for her interpretation of Mussorgsky's songs; author of *Le Legs de Moussorgsky* (1908); (her husband Baron Pierre d'Alheim (1862–1922) also wrote a book about the composer) she was a convinced Communist, selling *L'Humanité* on the streets of Paris; she died aged 101 in Moscow.

O'NEILL, Mrs Norman (Adine Rückert) (1875–1947) German pianist; pupil of Clara Schumann; head of music at St Paul's Girls' School, London 1903–37; gave many recitals in Britain.

PARNASSIENS, Les A group of French poets, hostile to Romantics such as Victor Hugo and Lamartine, and followers of the 'art for arts's sake' classical ideals of the *Pléiade* (*qv*); their works appeared 1866–76 in collections entitled *Le Parnasse contemporain*, named after the Greek mountain of Parnassus, sacred to Apollo and the Muses. The spiritual leader of the French Parnassians was Leconte de Lisle; other members of the group included Gautier, Hérédia, Catulle Mendès, Coppée and, to some degree, Villiers de l'Isle-Adam, Verlaine and Mallarmé, who were drawn towards the Symbolists (*qv*).

PASCAL STRING QUARTET French quartet formed in 1919 by André Pascal (1894–19?) who studied at Paris Conservatoire with Widor.

PÉGUY, Charles (1873–1914) French poet, playwright and essayist, killed in Battle of the Marne; devout Catholic and patriot but Dreyfusite, republican and in favour of international socialism. Of her Péguy record Croiza said that it was not good but not so bad that she must reject it; according to Hélène Abraham (*qv*) it must be played at 70 rpm, not at 78 rpm at which speed Croiza's voice is made to sound unnatural.

PLÉIADE, La   Two groups of French poets adopted the name, originally taken from the Pleiades constellation by seven poets during the years 285–247 BC, who lived in the reign of Ptolemy Philadelphus. The first and more important of the two French groups consisted of seven poets of the 16th century whose aim it was to enrich the French language by encouraging poets to write in their own tongue rather than Greek or Latin (the current practice) but at the same time to adopt the poets of antiquity as models, not translating or copying their works but imitating their style and form. The seven poets included Ronsard (*qv*) their spiritual leader, and Joachim du Bellay (*qv*), who published the group's manifesto in 1549. A second French group, of lesser importance, dates from the first half of the 17th century.

PONSELLE, Rosa (1897–1981)   American soprano; originally a vaudeville performer; operatic début 14 November 1918 in *La Forza del destino* with Caruso at the New York Met; her voice, technique and interpretative ability made her one of the outstanding sopranos of the century.

POULENC, Francis (1899–1963)   French composer, pianist and author; member of 'Les Six' (*qv*); from 1934 partner with Pierre Bernac (baritone) in duo for performance of songs of France and other countries; Croiza thought his songs had unusual tessitura, and were hard for the voice; Poulenc considered Croiza among his best interpreters, for *Le Bestiaire*; he dedicated 'Je n'ai plus que les os', from *Poèmes de Ronsard*, to her.

PRO ARTE STRING QUARTET   Belgian quartet, formed in 1912; from 1918 to 1939 its members were Alphonse Onnou, Laurent Halleux, Germain Prévost and Robert Maas; pre-eminent in classical and romantic music and in Haydn and 20th century music; it was one of the first ensembles to bring before the public avant-garde works by, for example, Hindemith, Schoenberg, Stravinsky, Honegger, Milhaud and Bartók (who dedicated his Fourth Quartet to it). It played at the first festival of the International Society for Contemporary Music at Salzburg in 1926 and at the concerts in 1926 inaugurating the Coolidge Auditorium in the Library of Congress in Washington.

PROUST, Marcel (1871–1922)   French novelist and writer on aesthetic subjects; in his youth regarded as a society dilettante; his immense novel *À la recherche du temps perdu* revealed him to have been a subtle, merciless observer of the psychological, moral and social behaviour of all classes of society.

RACINE, Jean (1639–69) French poet and dramatist in whose tragedies humanity is shown as being destroyed by the ambition, jealousy, vanity and passion which it harbours.

REDON, Odilon (1846–1916) French painter; influenced by Corot, Delacroix and Fantin-Latour; he aimed to involve the spectator by forcing him to search for the essential idea behind a painting, for example by including details which were absurd, out of scale or with ambiguous captions.

REEVES, George (1893–1960) British pianist; professor, Royal College of Music, London 1917–1919 and Urbana University (USA); début solo recital Wigmore Hall, London 1913; leading accompanist and chamber-music player with Calvé, Casals, Croiza, Melba, Schwarzkopf, Teyte, Thibaud etc.

RÉGNIER, Henri de (Henri-François Joseph de Régnier) (1864–1936) French neo-classical poet and novelist; originally a Parnassian, and close to Sully Prudhomme and Hérédia (whose daughter he married); later tended towards Symbolism under the influence of Mallarmé.

REICHEMBERG, Suzanne (1853–1924) French actress; entered Paris Conservatoire at 12; won first prize there 1868; same year Agnès in *Femmes savantes*; admired for her finesse and artistic purity in ingénue rôles throughout her career.

RÉJANE (pseud. of Gabrielle-Charlotte Réju) (1857–1920) French actress; though successful in emotional rôles she was particularly celebrated for her vivacity and for her performances as a comedienne.

RENARD, Jules (1864–1910) French poet and novelist; a moralist and acute observer of nature and of human behaviour. His best known works are the poems *Histoires naturelles* and the novel *Poil de Carotte*.

RESZKE, Jean de (Jan Mieczyslaw de Reszke) (1850–1925) Polish tenor and teacher; originally baritone; his teachers included Cotogni; début Venice 1874 in *La Favorita*; début as tenor Madrid 1879 in title rôle of *Robert le Diable*; first real success, due partly to Massenet's encouragement, was at Paris Opéra in 1884 as John the Baptist in première of *Hérodiade*; regarded as one of the supreme opera singers of the century; as teacher his pupils included Mme Charles Cahier, Arthur Endrèze, Miriam Licette, Maggie Teyte and — for one month — Croiza.

REVELLO, Adèle French singing teacher, conductor and pianist; of

Italian parentage; studied piano at Marseilles Conservatoire; taught at Paris Conservatoire from 1878; to prepare pupils for singing in opera, she gave repertoire classes in a large hall; inaugurated 'Théâtre Revello' 1879, herself conducting pupils in *Mireille*, *Galathée* etc. She was Croiza's first teacher for both voice and piano.

ROCHÉ, Henri-Pierre (18?–1960) French dilettante writer, critic and collector; had flair for discovering artists and writers of future importance such as Laurencin, Picasso, Gertrude Stein, Léautaud and the Surrealists, notably Marcel Duchamp; lived for periods in New York; editor of review *Ariane ou le pavillon dans le parc*; from English translations of ancient Chinese poetry by H. A. Giles (*qv*) Roché made versions in French set to music by Roussel; a 1961 film of François Truffaut's was based on Roché's *Jules et Jim*.

ROLLAND, Romain (1866–1944) French playwright, novelist and writer on musical, biographical and pacifist subjects; his anti-war position during the first world war was criticized.

RONSARD, Pierre de (1524–85) French poet of courtly love; influenced by classical models; the greatest French poet of the sixteenth century. With Joachim du Bellay and others he founded the *Pléiade* group (*qv*).

ROSTAND, Edmond (1868–1918) French playwright and poet; among his best known plays were *L'Aiglon*, written for Sarah Bernhardt, and *Cyrano de Bergerac*, in the première of which Coquelin *ainé* appeared in the title rôle.

ROUSSEL, Albert (1869–1937) French composer and teacher; originally a naval officer; studied with Gigout and d'Indy; among his pupils were Satie, Varèse and Martinů; he wrote four symphonies, the opera *Padmâvati*, *Évocations* for orchestra with chorus, about 35 songs, piano and chamber works and — his best known work — the ballet *Le Festin de l'araignée*.

SAMAIN, Albert (1858–1900) French neo-classical poet influenced by the Symbolists and Parnassians; one of the founders of the journal *Mercure de France*. Born into a petit-bourgeois family, he suffered privations leading to death from consumption.

SCHMITT, Florent (1870–1958) French composer; pupil of Dubois, Lavignac, Massenet and Fauré; prolific composer of songs, chamber music, works for piano, choir and orchestra; his best known works are the ballet *La Tragédie de Salomé* and a setting for choir and orchestra of Psalm 47.

SCHRÖDER-DEVRIENT, Wilhelmine (1804–60) German dramatic soprano; début 1821 as Pamina; her remarkable performance in Vienna in 1822 as Leonore in *Fidelio* helped to establish the opera in the repertoire; she sang in the premières of *Rienzi* and *The Flying Dutchman*.

SÉVERAC, Joseph Marie Déodat de (1873–1921)   French composer; pupil of Magnard and d'Indy at Schola Cantorum and, for piano, of Albeniz; wrote piano and orchestral music, songs and operas; devoted to the music of his native Languedoc, he sometimes wrote parts for regional folk instruments in his scores.

SILVESTRE, Armand (1837–1901)   French poet and art critic; one-time Inspecteur des Beaux-Arts; his poetry was admired by Fauré.

SIX, LES   During the first world war the composers Auric, Durey and Honegger were associated with Cendrars, Cocteau, Apollinaire and other writers in evenings devoted to music and poetry readings. The group, inspired by Satie, was known as 'Les Nouveaux Jeunes', and for some years it organized concerts with such artists as Jane Bathori, Ricardo Viñes and Hélène Jourdan-Morhange (*qv*); the original three composers were joined by Germaine Tailleferre, Darius Milhaud (*qv*) and Poulenc (*qv*) and, in 1920, the critic Henri Collet gave them the name 'Les Six'; this was a reference to 'The Five' — the group of Russian composers who rejuvenated the music of their country. Jean Cocteau was propagandist for 'Les Six'.

SOCIÉTÉ NATIONALE DE MUSIQUE   A society devoted to promoting works by its members, founded by Romain Bussine (*qv*) and Saint-Saëns in 1871; its first secretary was Alexis de Castillon and its second Fauré; it had a considerable influence on propagation of new music, particularly chamber music, in France.

SOUZAY, Gérard (pseud. of Gérard Michel Tisserand) (b.1918) French baritone; studied with Croiza, Bernac, Vanni Marcoux and others; his international career has embraced not only French opera and the *mélodie* but German opera and the *Lied*.

SUARÈS, André (pseud. of Félix André Yves Scantrel) (1868–1948)   French man of letters; attracted to Breton mysticism; wrote biographies of Cervantes, Goethe, Tolstoy and others, including Debussy, of whom he was a friend.

SULLY PRUDHOMME, René-François-Armand (1839–1907) French Parnassian poet; born into a wealthy family, he studied engineering and law but was able to devote himself to the classics and to philosophy and literature; he was a champion of Dreyfus.

SYMBOLISTS, The   Symbolism developed out of Parnassianism in the 1880s and was to some extent a reaction against the Parnassian ideals of clarity and precision; the Symbolists supported Wagner's idea of a synthesis of thought, emotion, poetry, art and music;

their goal was a poetry with the freedom, from literary or representational allusions, of pure music: a vehicle able to signify what could not be expressed. Symbolism in its extreme form as, for example, seen in the works of Villiers de l'Isle-Adam and Huysmans, was sometimes termed *décadent*; it was a forerunner of Surrealism.

The ancestors of Symbolism were Vigny, Baudelaire, Gérard de Nerval, Gautier and Banville; in its first phase its principal exponent was Verlaine; in its second Mallarmé, whose aesthetic theory provided its intellectual basis; apart from those mentioned the group also included Verhaeren, Rimbaud, Moréas, Laforgue, Régnier, Viélé-Griffin, Samain, Rémy de Gourmont, Montesquieu and Claudel.

TIERSOT, Jean-Baptiste Élisée Jullien (1857–1936)   French composer, musicologist and music editor; pupil of Massenet and Fauré at Paris Conservatoire of which he was later librarian; prolific writer on folklore and other musical subjects.

TOSCANINI, Arturo (1867–1957)   Italian conductor; trained as a cellist at Parma Conservatoire; conducted at Scala, Milan, from 1896, at the New York Met 1908–1915, with the NY Philharmonic-Symphony Orch. from 1926 and with the NBC Symphony Orch. (formed specially for his American broadcasts) 1937–1954; he also conducted at the Bayreuth and Salzburg festivals before the second world war; he was bitterly opposed to Fascism and the Nazis; he had poor eyesight and a memory described by Busoni as a 'phenomenon in the history of physiology'; his range of musical sympathies was exceptional and his repertoire enormous: he is known to have conducted some 600 works, including 117 operas, all rehearsed and conducted from memory. He was considered by many to have been supreme in the history of conducting.

TOULET, Paul-Jean (1867–1920)   French poet and author of satirical psychological novels; wrote a version of *As you like it* for abortive opera by Debussy.

VALÉRY, Paul (1871–1945)   French poet, critic and lecturer; his father was Corsican and his mother Italian; in 1891 he met Mallarmé, whose rigorous critical intelligence he admired; his range of interests was wide — art, science, philosophy, politics and, in particular, the nature of poetry and art and the psychology of the artist; from 1900 for many years he wrote no poetry, but the publication of *La Jeune Parque* in 1917 made his name; he was one of the most respected French men of letters of his time; it was

Valéry who interested Croiza in giving public recitations of poetry.

VAN LERBERGHE, Charles (1861–1907)   Belgian Symbolist and mystical poet and playwright.

VERLAINE, Paul (1844–96)   French poet, anti-romantic and Parnassian; in his youth in favour of order and clarity; in 1869 he met the 16 year old Mathilde de Mauté de Fleurville (1853–1914), his passion for her resulting in *La Bonne chanson* and other poems; they were married in 1870 but were legally separated 18 months later, Verlaine having left his wife for the young Rimbaud. In later years Verlaine's poetry became more innovative and more personal, though there was a final period of reversion to Catholicism and repentance.

VIARDOT, Pauline (Michelle Ferdinande Pauline Viardot-Garciá) (1821–1910)   French mezzo-soprano of Spanish parentage; daughter of the tenor Manuel del Popolo Vicente Garciá and sister of the famous voice teacher Manuel Patriccio Rodriguez Garciá and the singer Maria Malibran; studied singing with her parents, piano with Liszt and composition with Reicha; wrote operas for which Turgenev, who gave her lifelong devotion, wrote libretti; stage début Brussels 1837; created rôle of Fidès in Meyerbeer's *Le Prophète* in Paris 1849; her salon was a centre of intellectual life, frequented by Turgenev, Georges Sand, Flaubert, Saint-Saëns and Fauré, who dedicated two songs to her.

VILLE DE MIRMONT, Jean de la (Yan Alexandre Jean de la Ville de Mirmont) (1886–1914)   French poet killed in the first world war; his poems were set by Fauré in the short cycle *L'Horizon chimérique*.

VILLIERS DE L'ISLE ADAM, Philippe Auguste Mathias, Comte de (1838–89)   French poet and playwright; descended from a hero of the Crusades; was at the start of the Symbolist movement in France; the romantic idealism of his plays and poetry is a complete contrast to the poverty in which most of his life was spent; he was bitterly critical of the values of his time — science, progress and the love of money. He is remembered mainly by his mystical play *Axël*.

VILLON, François (1431–89)   the greatest French poet of the 15th century; as a young man he murdered a priest, was sentenced to death, but was pardoned; he committed other crimes and endured lifelong poverty and hardship; his poetry reflects compassion for the common people whose sufferings resemble those of his own misspent life.

Notes

Voснт, Louis de (Lodewijk de) (1887–1977)   Belgian conductor and composer; student and later professor and director of Antwerp Conservatoire; founded the Caecilia Choir (Chorale Sainte-Cécile) 1916 and was its conductor until 1967; conductor of the Concerts Classiques and Nouveaux Concerts in Antwerp; composer of songs, masses and other choral works, tone poems and a 'Symphonie pour choeurs et batterie'; played a leading part in introducing into Belgium works by Honegger, Milhaud, and other modern composers.

VOLTAIRE (pseud. of François-Marie Arouet) (1694–1738)   French moralist, dramatist, poet, satirist and historian; a deist campaigner against intolerance; universal genius.

VUILLERMOZ, Émile (1878–1960)   French music critic; composed operettas, songs etc. but abandoned composition in favour of criticism; pupil of Fauré at Paris Conservatoire at same time as Ravel, Enesco, Schmitt, Laparra and others; friend of Debussy; champion of modern music, writing *Musiques d'aujourd'hui* 1923; wrote biographies of Debussy and Fauré and many other books about music; a founder of *Société Musicale Indépendante* 1910 and editor of *SIM Revue musicale* from 1911.

WALTER, Bruno (pseud. of B. W. Schlesinger) (1876–1962)   German conductor and pianist; studied at Stern Conservatorium, Berlin; protégé of Mahler; one of the leading conductors of the age.

WATTEAU, Antoine (1684–1721)   The most important of French Rococo painters; scenes from the Italian Commedia dell' Arte are the subject matter of many of his paintings.

YSAŸE, Eugène (1858–1931)   Belgian violinist, composer and conductor; pupil of Massart, Wieniawski and Vieuxtemps. He established and conducted the Concerts Ysaÿe in Brussels and led the Ysaÿe String Quartet; he conducted the Cincinnati Symphony Orchestra 1918–22; one of the most celebrated violinists of his time, he gave first performances of many works, including Franck's Sonata (dedicated to him), Fauré's First Piano Quintet (with the composer) and Debussy's String Quartet (dedicated to the members of the Ysaÿe Quartet).

APPENDIX

Two letters from Duparc to Croiza
translated by Betty Bannerman

Tarbes (H^{tes} Pyr)
52 Rue Soult
17 October 1914

Mademoiselle,
I too am anxious to tell you what happiness your very kind visit
gave us: I should like to have written yesterday, but my poor sight
did not permit it, the day was so very dark. While you were here I
could not express the emotion and pleasure I had in hearing you;
music moves me *too much*, as I told you. When I feel that some of the
pages that I have written have been understood and interpreted in
such a way [as yours] I cannot prevent myself from thinking of all
those that I have not been able to write, and that would have been
sung so magnificently; and then, as soon as I want to say a word, I
feel my throat choking me.

Perhaps I was far too premature in promising to make a transposition of 'L'Invitation au voyage': I tried just now, and could not
do it. I do not know if, on a clearer day, my sight will permit it. In
any case, I will do my best, and I think the version in this key will
please you much more than the one in A minor. Moreover it is the
key I had chosen for printing in the transposed collection; but the
unfortunate Badaux, who was still alive, objected 'that people
would be frightened at the sight of 5 flats in the key signature'.
What an absurdity! Be that as it may, I let him have his way.

Please thank your most charming friend [Ivana Meedintiano],
and tell her that concerning her accompaniment about which she
was very wrong to excuse herself, I regret I am not at all of her
opinion: I find, on the contrary, that it was excellent; and I like
immensely this expressive way of accompanying, that follows and
envelops the voice like a garment, making one with it, that — in a

word — is not pianistic, but orchestral, from the heart and the intelligence.

I wanted to send your friend, as a souvenir of her visit to Tarbes, a little piece performed three years ago by Chevillard and whose transcription for piano was published a few months ago: but after having written 'à Mademoiselle . . .' I had to stop, realizing I did not know her name. Please have the great kindness to let me know what it is: I will send the minute piece at the same time as your transposition.

Please accept, dear Mademoiselle, to both of you, the new expression of my gratitude, and the homage of my most respectful feelings.

H. DUPARC

Please excuse, I pray you, my bad writing and my crossings out: the fault is in my eyes, that do not see the pen with which I write.

Tarbes (H^tes Pyr)
52 Rue Soult
14 April 1916

Dear Mademoiselle,

How very kind of you to have written your delightful and far too flattering letter! I was very much touched by it; only, let me reproach you for having no consideration for my vanity. Certainly, the few pages of music I have written do not deserve to be loved in the way they are; however, as they are, I am far from complaining, and am content to reflect how fortunate they are to be interpreted by such an artist as yourself.

If my poor eyesight, nearly non-existent, did not make journeys almost impossible for me, I would not have missed going to hear you; but unfortunately that was out of the question.

When you gave us the great — the very great — pleasure of coming to Tarbes, I did not dare to ask you to sing 'La Vie antérieure' and 'Le Testament', which you had just sung at Lyons and which are my favourites; though I wanted to do so I felt that I could not add to fatigue after the journey which you had been kind enough to make. Since then, I have often regretted this, and I tell myself that it would not have tired you at all and that it would have given me great pleasure; so I am warning you in advance: if ever I have the happiness of seeing you here again I shall not be so stupidly discreet. I even compliment you in advance on your admirable, perfect interpretation (for I know that is what it will be) and offer my profound gratitude.

Mme Duparc asks me to say that her memories of you remain with her both in her heart and on her back: for in spite of the season — it is true that since last night it has been perishingly cold — she is still wearing the charming and comfortable woolly that you gave her.

Accept, dear Mademoiselle, with the most affectionate memories, the expression of my feelings and my respectful and very grateful friendship.

H. DUPARC

P.S. Forgive my terrible scribble that you will probably have great difficulty in reading: would you believe I do not even see the pen I am using! Well! . . . I do what I can.

DISCOGRAPHY

BY PATRICK SAUL

Catalogue numbers are in bold type and matrix numbers in italics

French Columbia 12 inch (30cm)

D 15026 *LX 265*: Debussy: *Pelléas et Mélisande* (Maeterlinck), Act , Scene 2, La Lettre (with Armand Narçon, bass, and orchestra under Georges Truc) (recorded 6 March 1928) (also issued on UK Columbia L 2237) (in set from the opera on D 15021/4 and D 15026/7; UK L 2233/8, US 68518/23D) (Croiza sings Geneviève)

D 15041 *LX 363*: Duparc: L'Invitation au voyage (Baudelaire) (with Francis Poulenc, piano) (recorded 1928)

LX 328: Poulenc: Le Bestiaire (Apollinaire) (with composer, piano) (recorded 1928)

D 15129 *LX 657*: Roussel: Light, Op.19, No.1 (Jean-Aubry) (with composer, piano) (recorded 1928)

LX 682: Bréville: *Deux Rondels*: Adieu vous dy; Le Souvenir de vous me tue (attrib. to Villon) (with composer, piano) (recorded 1928)

D 15187 *LX 658*: Roussel: Invocation, Op.8, No.3 (Régnier) (with composer, piano) (recorded 1928)

LX 964: Bréville: Les Fées (Gauthier-Villars) (with composer, piano) (recorded 1928)

Honegger: *Judith*, biblical drama (René Morax)

D 15240 *52010* — Cantique Funèbre

52012 — Invocation, Fanfare et Incantation (recorded 1929)

D 15241 *WLBX 59* — Interlude et Cantique des vierges

52017 — Cantique de victoire (recorded 1929)

D 15241 *LX 717* — Retour de Judith et Cantique de la bataille (recorded 1928)

52017 — Cantique de victoire (recorded 1929)

(with Mlle. van Hertbruggen, Mme Is. van Dijck, the Chorale Caecilia, Antwerp, and the Orchestra of the Nouveaux Concerts, Antwerp, under Louis de Vocht). (NOTE Mme Croiza is heard only on sides 52012, 52017 and LX 717 of the three records listed above)

D 15243 *52013*: Milhaud: L'Orestie, 2: Les Choéphores, Op.24 (Aeschylus, translated by Claudel); Exhortation, Conclusion (with same forces as Honegger *Judith* above) (This is the second of two records from *Les Choéphores*, but Mme Croiza does not take part in D 15242) (recorded 1930)

LFX 109 *MX 5*: Debussy: Le Jet d'eau (Baudelaire) (with George Reeves, piano)
MX 6: Roussel: Jazz dans la nuit (Dommange) (with ditto)

French Columbia 10 inch (25 cm)

D 13032 *WL 686–2*: Schubert: An die Musik (in French) (with Eugène Wagner, piano) (recorded 1927)
L 683: Schubert: Wohin? (in French) (with ditto) (recorded 1927)
D 13033 *L 685*: Fauré: Clair de lune (Verlaine) (with Francis Poulenc, piano) (recorded 1927)
WL 722: Fauré: Prison (Verlaine) (with ditto) (recorded 1927)
D 13082 *WL 1329*: Roussel: Amoureux séparés (Roché, after Giles) (with composer, piano) (recorded 1928)
L 1295: Honegger: *Trois Chansons de la petite sirène* (Morax): Chanson des sirènes; Berceuse de la sirène (with composer, piano) (recorded 1928)
D 13082 *L 1295*: as on previous disc
L 1294: Honegger: *Six Poèmes d'Alcoöls* (Apollinaire): Automne (with composer, piano) (recorded 1928)
D 13084 *WL 1212*: Debussy: *Ariettes oubliées*, 2. Il pleure dans mon coeur (Verlaine) (with Francis Poulenc, piano) (recorded 1928)
L 1328: Roussel: Sarabande (Chalupt) (with composer, piano) (recorded 1928)
D 13085 *WL 1335*: Bréville: La Belle au bois (Lorrain) (with composer, piano) (recorded 1928)
WL 1334: Bréville: Une Jeune fille parle (Moréas) (with ditto) (recorded 1928)
LF 59 *M 37*: Duparc: Chanson triste (Lahor) (with George Reeves, piano) (recorded June 1930)
M 33: Duparc: Lamento (Gautier) (with ditto) (recorded June 1930)
LF 60 *M 35*: Séverac: Ma poupée chérie (Séverac) (with ditto) (recorded June 1930)
M 39: Séverac: Albado (Marguerite de Navarre) (with ditto) (recorded June 1930)
LF 61 *M 32*: Tiersot (harmonized): L'Amour de moy (anon) (with ditto) (recorded June 1930)
M 34: Vuillermoz (edited): Jardin d'amour (Vuillermoz) (with ditto) (recorded June 1930)
LF 63 *M 31*: Fauré: Soir (Samain) (with ditto) (recorded June 1930)
M 36: Fauré: Après un rêve (Bussine) (with ditto) (recorded June 1930)
unpublished *W 805–1*: Debussy: Ballade de Villon pour prier Nostre-Dame (with piano)
unpublished *WL 807–1*: Debussy: *Fêtes galantes*, series 2, No. 3, Colloque sentimental (Verlaine)
unpublished *WL 1057–1*: Poulenc: *Poèmes de Ronsard* No. 3, Ballet (with composer, piano) (recorded 1928)

unpublished *WL 1331–2*: Roussel: Le Jardin mouillé (Regnier) (with composer, piano) (recorded 1928 takes 1 and 2, 1929 take 3)

unpublished (conjectural): Roussel: À un jeune gentilhomme (Roché, after Giles)

Lumen 10 inch (25 cm)

30008 *XL 21–2*: Caplet: *Prières*, 1. Oraison dominicale (with Micheline Kahn, harp, and Pascal String Quartet)

XL 22: Caplet: *Prières*, 2. Salutation angélique (with ditto)

32045 *YL 91*: Debussy: Ballade de Villon pour prier Nostre-Dame (with Ivana Meedintiano, piano)

YL 92 { Debussy: Les Cloches (Bourget) (with ditto)
Debussy: Les Angélus (Le Roy) (with ditto)

35005 *YC 9*: Péguy: *Mystère des Saints Innocents*: Rien n'est beau comme un enfant qui s'endort en faisant sa prière (*spoken*) (recorded April 1934)

YC 10: Péguy: *Porche du mystère*, Ô Nuit, ô ma fille la nuit (*spoken*) (recorded April 1934)

35010 *YC 22–2*: Racine: *Esther*, Act I, scene 4, Ô mon souverain Roi (*spoken*) (recorded 1934)

YC 23–2: Racine: *Athalie*, Act 2, scene 5, Un songe (*spoken*) (recorded 1934)

Private Recordings

Honegger: *Quatre poèmes de Laforgue*: Petite chapelle (with composer, piano) (25 cm) (recorded 1929?)

Ravel: *L'Enfant et les sortilèges*: Air de l'enfant (with piano) (25 cm) (two versions) (recorded Paris, ?ca 1937)

Caplet: *Prières* (with piano) (25 cm) (recorded Paris, ?ca 1937)

Claudel: Pour la fête de Sainte Agnès; Minuit sonne; La Saint Martin (*spoken*) (25 cm) (recorded Paris, February 1938)

Claudel: La Vierge à midi; Le Chemin dans le domaine de l'idée et dans celui de l'art (*spoken*) (25 cm) (recorded Paris February 1938)

With the exception of the records with accompaniments played by George Reeves, which were recorded in London, all were recorded in Paris

NOTE There are several unusual features in the list of Croiza's records. Columbia D 13082 is found in two forms, as is D 15241. The seven Columbia records of passages from *Pelléas et Mélisande* (of which D 15026 or L 2237 is one) were issued in England with the consecutive numbers L 2233–8. In France they were numbered D 15021–4 and D 15026–7. Unfortunately D 15025 is not an unknown record by Croiza; it turns out to be 'Nuages', conducted by Gaubert.

Similarly, in the series LF 59–63, the missing LF 62 is not by Croiza; and D 13083 is sung by Fugère.

Long playing reissues (33 rpm)

1. The items marked in the composer index with a † were included on an LP prepared by Miss Betty Bannerman as CRO 1; this was later published by EMI as ALP 2115 and in Japan as Angel GR 2221.

2. *Le Bestiaire* (Poulenc) (Columbia D 15041) has appeared on the following Pathé-Marconi records: C 047–12538 (entitled *Francis Poulenc: pianiste et accompagnateur*), COLC 317 and C 051–14150.

3. Extracts from *Pelléas et Mélisande* (Debussy), (including the Letter scene sung by Croiza), has been issued on Pearl GEMM 145.

COMPOSER INDEX

Bréville (all with the composer, piano)
La Belle au bois. Columbia D 13085
Les Fées. Columbia D 15187
†Une Jeune fille parle. Columbia D 13085
Deux Rondels: Adieu vous dy; Le Souvenir de vous me tue. Columbia D 15129

Caplet
Les Prières: Oraison dominicale; Salutation angélique (with Micheline Kahn, harp, and Pascal String Quartet). Lumen 30008
Les Prières (unidentified) (with piano) private recording

Debussy
Les Angélus (with Ivana Meedintiano, piano) Lumen 32045
Ballade de Villon pour prier Nostre-Dame (with ditto) Lumen 32045
Ditto (with unidentified accompaniment) Columbia unpublished *W 805–1*
Les Cloches (with Ivana Meedintiano, piano) Lumen 32045
Colloque sentimental (*Fêtes galantes*, series 2, No.3) (with piano acc.) Columbia unpublished *WL 807–1*
†Il pleure dans mon coeur (*Ariettes oubliées*, No.2) (with Francis Poulenc, piano) Columbia D 13084
†Le Jet d'eau (with George Reeves, piano) Columbia LFX 109
†*Pelléas et Mélisande*, Act 1, scene 2, La lettre (with Armand Narçon, bass, and orchestra under Georges Truc) Columbia D 15026

Duparc
†Chanson triste (with George Reeves, piano) Columbia LF 59
†L'Invitation au voyage (with Francis Poulenc, piano) Columbia D 15041
†Lamento (with George Reeves, piano) Columbia LF 59

Fauré
†Après un rêve (with George Reeves, piano) Columbia LF 63
Clair de lune (with Francis Poulenc, piano) Columbia D 13033
Prison (with ditto) Columbia D 13033
†Soir (with George Reeves, piano) Columbia LF 63

Honegger
†*Trois Chansons de la petite sirène*: Chanson des sirènes; Berceuse de la sirène (with the composer, piano) Columbia D 13082
Six Poèmes d'Alcoöls: Automne (with ditto) Columbia D 13082

Judith, biblical drama: Invocation, Fanfare et Incantation; Cantique de victoire; Retour de Judith et Cantique de la bataille (with Chorale Caecilia, Antwerp, Orchestra of the Nouveaux Concerts, Antwerp under Louis de Vocht) Columbia D 15240/1

Quatre Poèmes de Laforgue: Petite chapelle (with the composer, piano) private recording

Milhaud

L'Orestie, 2: *Les Choéphores*, Op.24: Exhortation; Conclusion (with same forces as Honegger: *Judith* (see above) Columbia D 15243

Poulenc

Poèmes de Ronsard: No.3, Ballet (with the composer, piano) Columbia unpublished *WL 1507–1*

†*Le Bestiaire* (with ditto) Columbia D 15041

Ravel

L'Enfant et les sortilèges: Air de l'enfant (with piano) 2 separate private recordings

Roussel

À un jeune gentilhomme. Columbia unpublished (conjectural)

†Amoureux séparés (with the composer, piano) Columbia D 13082

†Invocation (with ditto) Columbia D 15187

Le Jardin mouillé (with ditto) Columbia unpublished (2 takes) *WL 1331–2*

†Jazz dans la nuit (with George Reeves, piano) Columbia LFX 109

†Light (with the composer, piano) Columbia D 15129

†Sarabande (with ditto) Columbia D 13084

Schubert

An die Musik (sung in French; with Eugène Wagner, piano) Columbia D 13032

Wohin? (sung in French; with ditto) Columbia D 13032

Séverac

Albado (with George Reeves, piano) Columbia LF 60

†Ma poupée chérie (with ditto) Columbia LF 60

Tiersot

L'Amour de moy (with George Reeves, piano) Columbia LF 61

Vuillermoz

Jardin d'amour (with ditto) Columbia LF 61

INDEX

BY PATRICK SAUL

Details of individual songs, song cycles, authors of texts, etc. are usually given under names of composers.
'n' preceding a page number indicates a reference to the Notes and 'd' a reference to the Discography.

Claire Croiza: The Singer as Interpreter

Index

Index

Index

Index